MODERN DRAMATISTS

Macmillan Modern Dramatists
Series Editors: *Bruce King* and *Adele King*

Published titles
Gerry McCarthy, *Edward Albee*
Theodore Shank, *American Alternative Theatre*
Bernard F. Dukore, *American Dramatists 1918–1945*
Frances Gray, *John Arden*
Michael Billington, *Alan Ayckbourn*
Charles R. Lyons, *Samuel Beckett*
David L. Hirst, *Edward Bond*
Ronald Speirs, *Bertolt Brecht*
Julian Hilton, *Georg Büchner*
Laurence Senelick, *Anton Chekhov*
Frances Gray, *Noel Coward*
Helen Keyssar, *Feminist Theatre*
Bettina L. Knapp, *French Theatre 1918–1939*
Dennis Walder, *Athol Fugard*
Jeannette L. Savona, *Jean Genet*
Renate Benson, *German Expressionist Drama*
Nick Worrall, *Nikolai Gogol and Ivan Turgenev*
Charles Hayter, *Gilbert and Sullivan*
David Thomas, *Henrik Ibsen*
Claude Schumacher, *Alfred Jarry and Guillaume Apollinaire*
Leonard C. Pronko, *Eugène Labiche and Georges Feydeau*
Reed Anderson, *Federico Garcia Lorca*
Dennis Carroll, *David Mamet*
Neil Carson, *Arthur Miller*
Ruby Cohn, *New American Dramatists 1960–80*
John Bull, *New British Political Dramatists*
Denis Calandra, *New German Dramatists*
Jan McDonald, *The 'New' Drama 1900–1914*
James Simmons, *Sean O'Casey*
Normand Berlin, *Eugene O'Neill*
Maurice Charney, *Joe Orton*
Bernard F. Dukore, *Harold Pinter*
Susan Bassnett-McGuire, *Luigi Pirandello*
Glenda Leeming, *Poetic Drama*
Arthur Ganz, *George Bernard Shaw*
James Gibbs, *Wole Soyinka*
Thomas R. Whitaker, *Tom Stoppard*
Margery Morgan, *August Strindberg*
Eugene Benson, *J. M. Synge*
Katharine Worth, *Oscar Wilde*
Roger Boxill, *Tennessee Williams*

Further titles are in preparation

MACMILLAN MODERN DRAMATISTS

POETIC DRAMA

Glenda Leeming

First published 1989

Published by
Higher and Further Education Division
MACMILLAN PUBLISHERS LTD
Houndmills, Basingstoke, Hampshire RG21 2XS
and London
Companies and representatives
throughout the world

Typeset by Wessex Typesetters
(Division of The Eastern Press Ltd)
Frome, Somerset

Printed in China

British Library Cataloguing in Publication Data
Leeming, Glenda
Poetic drama.—(Macmillan modern
dramatists)
1. Verse drama, English—History and
criticism 2. English drama—20th century
—History and criticism
I. Title
822'.912'09 PR739.V42
ISBN 0–333–36902–5
ISBN 0–333–36903–3 Pbk

Contents

List of Plates

Editors' Preface

The *Macmillan Modern Dramatists* is an international series of introductions to major and significant nineteenth and twentieth-century dramatists, movements and new forms of drama in Europe, Great Britain, America and new nations such as Nigeria and Trinidad. Besides new studies of great and influential dramatists of the past, the series includes volumes on contemporary authors, recent trends in the theatre and on many dramatists, such as writers of farce, who have created theatre 'classics' while being neglected by literary criticism. The volumes in the series devoted to individual dramatists include a biography, a survey of the plays, and detailed analysis of the most significant plays, along with discussion, where relevant, of the political, social, historical and theatrical context. The authors of the volumes, who are involved with theatre as playwrights, directors, actors, teachers and critics, are concerned with the plays as theatre and discuss such matters as performance, character interpretation and staging, along with themes and contexts.

BRUCE KING
ADELE KING

Acknowledgements

The author and publishers wish to thank the following who have kindly given permission for the use of copyright material:

Associated Book Publishers Ltd. for extracts from *Theatre at Work* by C. Marowitx and S. Trussler, Methuen 1967.
Cambridge University Press for extracts from *The Making of T. S. Eliot's Plays* by E. Martin Browne, 1969
Faber and Faber Ltd. for extracts from *Murder in the Cathedral*, *Family Reunion*, *The Cocktail Party*, *The Confidential Clerk*, *The Elder Statesman*, 'Sweeney Agonistes', 'Choruses from "The Rock"' and 'Gerontion' by T. S. Eliot; and Harcourt Brace Jovanovich, Inc., for extracts from *Murder in the Cathedral*, *Family Reunion*, *The Cocktail Party*, *The Confidential Clerk* and 'Sweeney Agonistes' by T. S. Eliot
David Higham Associates Ltd. on behalf of the author and New Directions Publishing Corporation for an extract from *Under Milk Wood* by Dylan Thomas. Copyright in US 1954 by New Directions Publishing Corporation
Southern Illinois University Press for extracts from

Joseph Hollway's Abbey Theatre: A Selection from his Unpublished Journal Impressions of a Dublin Playgoer edited by Robert Hogan and Michael J. O'Neill, 1967

A. P. Watt Ltd. on behalf of Michael Yates and Macmillan Publishing Company for extracts from *The Valiorum Edition* of the plays of W. B. Yeats, edited by Russell K. Alspach, 1966. Copyright in US 1921, 1924, 1928, 1934, 1935, 1951 by Macmillan Publishing Company. Copyright 1938 by William Butler Yeats. Copyright 1922, 1924 by The Dial Publishing Company. Copyrights renewed 1949, 1950, 1952, 1956, 1962 by Bertha Georgie Yeats. Copyright © Russell K. Alspach and Bertha Georgie Yeats 1966.

Every effort has been made to trace all the copyright holders but if any have been inadvertently overlooked the publishers will be pleased to make the necessary arrangement at the first opportunity.

1
Introduction: Poetic Drama and the Twentieth Century

> . . . the forms of drama are so various that few critics are able to hold more than one or two in mind pronouncing judgement of 'dramatic' and 'undramatic'.
>
> T. S. Eliot (SE 75)

Poetic drama has a long and respectable history, so much so that surveys of its twentieth-century practitioners tend to begin with discussions of the parameters laid down by critics from Aristotle to Dryden. However, classical poetics is of limited relevance to modern practice: whereas the Renaissance dramatists in Britain were working within a strong tradition of verse drama, against the background of surviving classical works in verse and the native heritage of religious and morality plays, also in verse, this tradition did not persist to the present. Though verse drama continued to be written and revived after the seventeenth century, its dominance as a creative force declined, and this eclipse was of great importance to the Poetic Drama Movement of the late nineteenth and early twentieth centuries. First, there was no vital, continuing verse drama form, so that would-be verse dramatists had no close models to develop or react against; and second, the nineteenth-century preoccupation with realism and naturalism in the arts undermined the conventions of theatre that were necessary for a non-naturalistic style of dramatic writing, which meant that verse dramatists had to reinvent conventions that would suit their work.

This exploratory new beginning for poetic drama meant that there was not strictly speaking a 'poetic drama movement' as such, but several dramatists at different times and different places writing plays in verse. What they had in common was a reaction against the conventional realism of current commercial theatre writing, and a willingness to experiment with relating form and content to the twentieth century, instead of limply imitating Shakespeare. The differences between the individual writers are more striking than the similarities, but there were relationships and influences, and increasingly the dramatists were aware of modern poetic drama as a distinct genre, little though they would agree on any common body of rules or aims.

William Butler Yeats (1865–1939), the pioneer of this diffuse movement, was the first to rethink structure, content and verse form in a way that set his work apart from the occasional vaguely historical verse plays of the nineteenth century. Unlike most of the other poetic dramatists, he worked with a permanent though changing group of actors, a company which eventually founded and settled at the Abbey Theatre, Dublin, and where there was at least some opportunity for him to control the productions of his plays. Sceptical and non-fanatical himself, Yeats was committed to the development of Irish culture and the sense of national identity. Hence most of his plays take their themes from Irish myth, such as the legend of Deirdre or the cycle dealing with the mythic hero Cuchulain. His actors were actually dedicated to the cause of Irish culture, and this and their amateur origins meant that they let Yeats experiment with obviously uncommercial themes and styles, such as deliberately still posing, stage tableaux, and semi-musical intoning of the verse lines in the 'tapestry like' *The Countess Cathleen* and *The Shadowy Waters*. In spite of the Irishness of his subject matter, Yeats was also influenced by European and Oriental drama. These static early plays show his interest in the dream-like atmospheric evocation of emotion by the Symbolist poets and particularly in the plays of Maeterlinck and Villiers de l'Isle Adam which he had seen in Paris. Later he was to imitate the abstract staging, using screens and lighting as non-representational background, designed by Edward Gordon Craig, and later still be modelled his plays on his own interpretation of the 'aristocratic' Noh plays of Japan. *At the Hawk's Well*, and *The Only Jealousy of Emer* are the most typical of these 'plays for dancers' which require highly formalised staging with masks, dancer and chorus of musicians. His modification of the Noh form in *Purgatory* – still spare, but no masks and no dancer – is one of his most successful and impressive works, but it is fair to say that Yeats was never able to command a large and steady audience, and his plays are seldom revived, whereas the more realistic prose dramatists nurtured by the Abbey, Synge and O'Casey, have found an established place in the repertoire.

Thomas Stearns Eliot (1888–1964), paid tribute to Yeats's experiments – 'Yeats had nothing, and we have had Yeats'[1] – but there are few evident lines of development from the older poet to the younger. Eliot's first and unfinished piece of dramatic writing, *Sweeney Agonistes* (1927), with its syncopated verse rhythms and colloquial style is quite unlike Yeats's early lyricism or his later terseness. And the fragments of *Sweeney*, though modern, are far from realistic, with the short rhyming exchanges and occasional songs. Similarly, Eliot's second venture into playwriting was different from his first, but was equally non-realistic and still owed nothing to Yeats. This time Eliot was supported by the movement for religious drama. Two trends in religious drama had emerged since the turn of the century – one was the wave of mainly amateur writing for church festivals and local religious celebrations, and the other, which fuelled the first, was a revival of interest in staging mediaeval mystery plays. Within this context, Eliot was asked to write the verse choruses and some dialogue scenes for what was loosely called a 'pageant play' – an episodic history of centuries of church building, produced at Sadlers Wells theatre to raise money for building new suburban churches. This play, *The Rock* (1934), was a kind of trial run for *Murder in the Cathedral* and the professional theatre, and gave Eliot his first experience of working for the stage, without the pressures of economics or theatrical fashion. However, his scenario was laid down by others, his actors were a huge group of unknown amateurs, and a committee of several other people were all involved in devising the final shape of the work, and therefore Eliot did not have the autonomy or the freedom to fail which Yeats had had, and this perhaps laid the foundation of his subsequent cautious aproach to dramatic creativity.

Murder in the Cathedral (1935) was the most significant and successful play produced under the shelter of the religious drama movement, and proved Eliot's dramatic gifts. In it, he used the re-enactment of a sacrifice as the deep structure of his play, based on the belief that the origins of serious drama lay in religious ritual, and this ritual aspect was reinforced by transformations of liturgy and sermon into the lyric chorus of Women of Canterbury and the direct addresses to the audiences which punctuate the dramatic depiction of the murder of Thomas à Becket. The emotional impact of this carried over to the theatre – the play transferred to the West End in the first of many commercial productions. But the special conditions – in the financial and professional sense – of the religious festival play meant that Eliot, and other writers for the genre, did not have to consider, for example, the economic necessity to provide a small cast, or to attract audiences by writing a number of star parts. Eliot himself felt that the festival audience would be psychologically prepared to extend indulgence towards more demanding verbal expression and archaic features, such as the use of a chorus. (Yeats had sardonically remarked of a friend's verse play: 'Many people have said to me that the surroundings of *Helena* made them feel religious. Once get your audience in that mood, and you can do anything with it'.[2])

Many other writers were also asked to contribute to religious festivals, and particularly after *Murder in the Cathedral* had shown the way, took advantage of the new assumption that religious drama was a non-realistic branch of theatre for which non-realistic dialogue was appropriate – and for most of these, such as Anne Ridler and Charles Williams, this meant writing in verse. The religious drama movement could then be seen as a releasing influence on playwriting at this time, and the example of Eliot offered new ideas to young writers such as Christopher Fry.

But at the same time, during the 1930s, as Eliot was

developing his own style, another and different trend in verse drama emerged. This was the political and social drama of Wystan Hugh Auden (1907–73) and Christopher Isherwood (1904–85) which took issues such as fascism, militarism or international competitiveness and dramatised them in an eclectic mixture of prose and different verse rhythms. Auden and Isherwood were influenced by 1930s Berlin cabaret sketches, and the satire was directed against contemporary social and ethical behaviour: they had little interest in exploring man's spiritual and imaginative life, and in this their aims and subject matter as well as their style were alien to both Yeats and Eliot. Nonetheless, Auden and Isherwood were just as much outside the prosperous mainstream of West End theatre as were the religious festivals or Yeats's original amateur group. They began writing for the little Group Theatre whose founder Rupert Doone was experienced and enthusiastic in the current experiments of the Parisian avant-garde, as regards colourful surreal sets and costumes, and the mixture of dance, music and dialogue. The theatrical effect of the early plays *The Dance of Death* (1933) and *The Dog Beneath the Skin* (1936) was visually bright and fast-moving, but the crudely expressed content appeared shallow, and unfortunately attempts to increase significance in *The Ascent of F6* (1936) and *On the Frontier* (1938) led to portentousness rather than complexity and in the process lost much of the original inventiveness and visual appeal. As the verse also diminished, the authors' ambitions to achieve success in the commercial theatre were discouraged, and their fellow poets MacNeice and Spender likewise made only single attempts at social playwriting before returning to lyric poetry or different forms of theatrical writing.

Meanwhile Eliot also was turning his attention to the

West End, inaugurating a phase in which poetic drama became fashionable and bankable in the commercial theatre. He had several reasons for this, of which the wish to make money played only a small part, if any. In a general sense, his belief that British cultural life would be improved by the promotion of poetic drama has something in common with Yeats's concern for Irish culture. This raising of the overall cultural level demanded that verse plays must be seen by the widest possible audiences, and this meant those going to the big West End theatres. Moreover, Eliot was anxious about the wholeheartedness or otherwise of the acceptance of the fringe religious drama, fearing that, as Yeats had said, the plays were praised for their moral purpose rather than for their theatrical qualities: 'people who go deliberately to a religious play at a religious festival expect to be patiently bored and to satisfy themselves with the feeling that they have done something meritorious' (SP 76). If poetic drama could justify its existence on its own merits, then the plays must stand on their own as plays and compete with realistic prose dramas on the same terms. And this necessarily affected the way that he wrote his next plays.

Public awareness of poetic drama was high during the post-war period of the 1940s and early 1950s; this was the stage at which it seemed that writers were beginning to produce popular, original plays which also deserved literary and philosophical approval and would be worthy to stand by the classic drama of the past. This was what Eliot had been hoping for, though his first play in a modern setting, *The Family Reunion* (1939), did not have a long run – partly due to the imminent outbreak of the Second World War, but partly also to its obscure message. However, *The Cocktail Party* (1949) though similarly baffling to some, was successful both in London and New

York, and these plays are still commercially revived. To some extent, then, Eliot's hopes were justified; the serious themes of the plays did appeal to audiences originally and increasingly as familiarity made them seem less obscure. Compared with *Murder in the Cathedral* with its choral grouping and colourful robed figures in numinous ecclesiastical setting, the modern plays visually were less striking – the characters in evening dress conversed in country house or smart flat as in any contemporary problem play – but the incantatory rhythms and compelling imagery emerged at least some of the time to insist on spiritual, non-materialistic issues *unlike* the issues of the problem play.

But the attention Eliot paid to what he thought his audiences would expect led to his progressive simplification of his verse style and to a diminishing of its poetic qualities. He aimed at a fairly realistic style in set, behaviour and dress, supposing this to be more acceptable to audiences, and tried to bring some of his verse dialogue into conformity with this realism. This effect is already occasionally apparent in *The Cocktail Party*, but in Eliot's last two plays, *The Confidential Clerk* (1953) and *The Elder Statesman* (1958), prosaic vocabulary and predictable word order is pervasive. These plays were tepidly received when first produced and have subsequently been neglected, and it seems likely that, as Eliot himself suspected, in fearing to put in too much poetry, he put in too little for his audience's taste.

The career of Christopher Fry (1907–) suggests that this may have been so: Fry's relation to Eliot is evident in his religious festival plays and in his use of non-Shakespearian verse in his modern as well as his historic plays. Some of the religious plays, were, like Eliot's, more innovative in technique – again, the sense of freedom from audience expectation given by the religious festival play genre seems to have been a releasing factor – but, at least in the earlier examples, his secular comedies did not attempt to modify their verse into a realistic imitation of ordinary conversation. *A Phoenix Too Frequent* (1946) was Fry's first characteristic comedy, and its immediate success with audiences owed much to the thickly clustered imagery and word play, though the fact that this play is set in Ancient Greece, and that his next comedy, *The Lady's Not For Burning* (1948), takes place in '1400, either more or less or exactly', could support Eliot's view that poetry is easily accepted from characters in historical costume. However, the action of Fry's equally popular *Venus Observed* (1950) unfolds in a present-day ducal mansion (granted that this is not the most insistently contemporary of settings) and still makes no concessions towards an illusion of realistic speech. It may have been coincidental that Fry's style did become more subdued, in that the images were less startling and less frequent and the alliterative, assonantal qualities of the dialogue became less noticeable, as his prominence in the theatre began to decline.

The new verse drama, with the names of Eliot and Fry bracketed as its leaders, seemed to be losing internal momentum at the same time as it was overtaken by newer movements, as British theatre discovered Absurd drama in the mid 1950s and the different styles of Ionesco, Genet and Beckett, while the socially conscious plays of Osborne, Wesker and Pinter reverted to material concerns and realistic presentation. By comparison with the wildly unpredictable absurdists the poetic dramatists seemed little different from the conventional realistic drawing-room comedy writers with whom they were competing, and at the same time the initial naturalism of the British New Wave made Eliot and Fry appear stilted and artificial. Concentrating on breaking into commercial theatre, Eliot never seems to have looked back towards his earlier experiments, but Fry's later works include the surreal dream-based *A Sleep of Prisoners* (1951) and the loosely episodic *Curtmantle* (1962); potentially there could have been a transition to verse plays within the absurdist framework, but Fry was not in tune with that world view, and the West End phase of the poetic drama movement closed there.

The early death of Dylan Thomas (1914–53) terminated another promising line of development, as his radio play *Under Milk Wood* (1954) uses a heightened, image-packed prose in its dialogue and narrative descriptive passages, which makes an easy transition to the recited verse and sung ballads he incorporates. Because the scenes are evoked verbally in a dream-like sequence in the mind of the blind narrator, Thomas can use exaggeration and cross-cutting and escape the limits of realism in action and expression. Again the continuing popularity of this work in its original radio version shows that audiences, far from shunning poetic theatrical dialogue, are enthusiastic about its undisguised and imaginative presentation.

Commonwealth dramatists such as Wole Soyinka (1934–), and Derek Walcott (1930–) developed the verse play more persistently, but in Britain the all-verse play is now rare. Tony Harrison (1937–) in his poetic versions of great plays of the past, such as the *Oresteia* and mediaeval mystery plays, has assumed the privilege of historic period for his language and thereby pushed the boundaries of poetic expression further away from ordinary speech. But the most significant use of verse in drama now is as one element in an often socially concerned, partly prose play. The twentieth-century reaction against realism has continued after the first wave of modernism, in theatre as in all the arts, and acceptance of various non-realistic features, such as direct address to the audience, mask, caricature, and song and dance, has widened from minority audiences to West End and provincial theatregoers.

European Background: Verse and Poetic Prose

It was not only English-speaking dramatists who experimented with poetic drama in various forms. Several individual European poets chose to write plays, and several influential movements included verse as one of their many new techniques. Yeats was at first the exception in seeking inspiration in European sources, as well as in his native Irish tradition. He selected carefully what he needed: his taste was already for strong atmosphere and static visual effects, and he became enthusiastic about the works of Villiers de L'Isle Adam, recognising these same qualities in them. Yeats met Maurice Maeterlinck in 1895 when he came to London for a production of his *The Intruder* (1891) and *Pelleas and Melisande* (1893); the latter exemplifies many of Maeterlinck's characteristic features, in a plot dealing with tension and half-admitted feelings between a man, his wife and his brother, set in a nebulous historical period. What makes this banal triangle Maeterlinckian is the strange isolation and introspection of the characters – the wife, Melisande, is found in the forest, has little explanation of her presence there or her previous life, and most of her speeches are short broken protests. The characters go wandering in subterranean tunnels; there is a cave with unexplained beggars in it. The dream atmosphere is expressionist in catching the imagination with foreboding, but having no clear-cut motivation or key to the free-floating emotion.

Maeterlinck wrote in prose, and his language by its scantiness builds tension and emphasises the unspoken: it is minimal dialogue, the characters usually uttering not lines of dialogue but half-lines, interrupting their longer speeches with pauses and hesitations. It is not poetry, but it is heavily significant literary language. Then, a generation or so later, equal intensity is offered by Federico García Lorca (1898–1936) who used a mixture of prose and poetry. His three best known 'folk tragedies' are tragically inevitable in a way that is almost extinct in modern drama. His *Blood Wedding* (1933) for example has no release of tension through comic relief or social commentary. The bride elopes with her married former sweetheart in a spirit of despair: they are driven by their physical attraction almost grudgingly and against any hope of success, to make the gesture of defying the iron-hard laws of their society. Just before the fleeing sweetheart and pursuing bridegroom kill each other, Lorca includes a strange sequence in which the Moon, as a young woodcutter, speaks a vampire-like song to Death, as an old woman. The lovers also express their despairing love in verse full of intense images of blood, broken glass, nails, stones, fire.

Between the vague emotion of Maeterlinck and the violent emotion of Lorca lies the more traditional approach of Claudel and Rostand, born in the same year, 1868. Claudel has been compared to T. S. Eliot in that his standpoint is religious, and he came to drama after establishing himself as a lyric poet. All the dialogue in his best-known play, *Break of Noon*, written in 1905 but not produced until 1948, is in verse but there is also a heightened monologue or 'song' for the protagonist Mesa, which requires semi-operatic powers in the actor – possibly it is something like what Yeats was once aiming at, though he could not have known this play. However, where Eliot's characters paled beneath the weight of their spiritual significance, Jean-Louis Barrault as Mesa and Edwige Feuillère as Yse projected the magnetic physical situation of lovers caught in another triangular relationship so powerfully as to overshadow the metaphysical framework. Other plays by Claudel such as *The Satin Slipper* (1924) were even less conventional in subject and form, but his development may have been hindered by his wandering life as a successful diplomat.

Rostand also wrote verse plays unmixed with prose, and reached the stage earlier in life, having an intimate insight into the workings of the professional theatre from his relationship with Sarah Bernhardt. In 1895 his *The Faraway Princess* was a failure, in spite of the divine Sarah playing the very unMaeterlinckian princess Mellisande, but his witty, imaginative verse play *Cyrano de Bergerac* (1897) was a great success. Verbal charm and inventiveness, highly valued in French drama, was further exploited in prose by Giraudoux (1882–1944) and Anouilh (1910–). Anouilh had in fact started to imitate Rostand's verse as a child, and later learnt from Giraudoux that theatre language could be, as he said, poetic and artificial and yet truer than stenographic conversation. This quality of brilliance both in Rostand's verse and in Giraudoux's and Anouilh's prose was most successful in England when translated by the brilliant and non-naturalist poet Christopher Fry.

The less polished drama of the Surrealists mixed some verse with the strong visual and auditory effects that Cocteau insisted were also 'poetry of the theatre'. Yeats had been dismayed by the vigorous assertiveness of Alfred Jarry's seminal *Ubu Roi* (1896), after attending its riotous first night:

> Feeling bound to support the most spirited party, we have shouted for the play, but that night at the Hotel Corneille I am very sad, for comedy, objectivity, has displayed its growing power once more . . . after our own verse, after the faint mixed tints of Conder, what more is possible? After us the Savage God.[3]

Against a background depicting side by side apple blossom, a fireplace, a skeleton, Jarry's bizarre characters spoke a crude functional prose, but other plays in this vein were more experimental in language too, such as Tristan Tzara's *Gas Heart* (1920) where the rhythmic, often nonsensical lines sometimes break into rhyme.

Fuller use of verse, however, is made by the German Expressionist dramatists. They were social visionaries rather than documentary writers, and often made their effects by association and symbol. Like the Surrealists, they explored no-realistic theatrical devices: animal masks, simultaneous staging, costumes of skeletons and angels were common, though used in a structured, less chaotic way. Sorge, in *The Beggar* (1912), for instance, used tableaux and choral group scenes to make a social comment, and some of these, such as his row of newspaper readers, are very similar to scenes in Auden's *On the Frontier*. Ernst Toller was less eclectic, and his episodic, sometimes dreamlike short scenes progressively build up the traumatic but instructive experience of his protagonists. His verse varies in form, but his favourite short line emphasises the gnomic, stark meaning of their perceptions. Auden translated some of Toller's work, and both form and content point forward to Brecht's plays.

The drama of Brecht was not, after the very early plays, part of the Expressionist school. The approach he took to verse, usually in ballad or song form, was to separate the different forms of speech from each other very sharply: in *The Good Person of Szechuan* (1943) Shen Teh sometimes addresses the audience directly in verse; in *The Caucasian Chalk Circle* (1949) the courtship between Grusha and her admirer is marked as a special, important transaction by being spoken in the formal third person, as different from the 'ordinary' dialogue as the verse is. In *Mother Courage* (1941) the many songs are narrative, each having a parallel but unobtrusive relevance to the main plot. The fashion for inserting 'Brechtian' songs or verses in plays in the 1960s and later was useful in showing the various possibilities of mixing styles in this way.

The influence of these European writers and others in these movements was a dual one. Some British dramatists of the early twentieth century found productive ideas in their work and absorbed these into their own plays; then later the interest in the (mainly prose) Absurd drama in the 1950s and early 1960s reawakened curiosity about its Surrealist and Expressionist forebears, and revivals demonstrated that experiments with language, along with other techniques, could form a valid part of modern plays of a very wide range of types.

The Theoretic Background

It is tempting to see the rejection of realism as the key to successful poetic drama, but this is obviously too simple to embrace all the different approaches to writing dramatic verse. Looking back over the various initiatives in the field, one can see at every stage a jealous tension between the poets' efforts to demonstrate the greater potentialities of verse, and their recognition of the still considerable range and undeniable popularity of realistic prose drama.

Initially most of the debutant dramatic poets recognised the problem of rejecting realism. Yeats immediately decided that non-realistic language required a consistent non-realistic convention for the other aspects of presentation: 'for poetry is founded upon convention, and becomes incredible the moment painting or gesture reminds us that people do not speak in verse when they meet upon the highway'. Eliot too was quite aware of the importance of convention; as he said about his *Murder in the Cathedral*:

> In watching a stage performance the member of the audience is in direct contact with the actor, is always conscious that he is looking at a stage and listening to an actor playing a part. In looking at a film. . . . We are seized with the illusion that we are observing the actual event.[4]

Auden equally assumed that film, by taking over the job of mere realistic imitation, would have the liberating effect on theatre that photography had had on painting:

> The development of the film has deprived drama of any excuse for being documentary. It is not in its nature to provide an ignorant and passive spectator with exciting news.[5]

But having made this point, the writers proceeded to

vary widely in interpreting the meaning of 'convention' and how far it was to go. Yeats appropriated considerable freedom of himself, paying little attention to the expectations to his audience. He was perfectly willing to invent stage settings, style of movement and method of speaking, as well as the dramatic dialogue, aiming to unite all these to create a particular atmosphere and effect, and not to remind the audience of anything in their own lives. Auden made a different but parallel appeal for 'acrobatics, dancing, and all forms of physical skill' as the basis for theatrical performance. On the other hand, Eliot thought of stage conventions as the medium through which, if necessary, an imitation of everyday life could appear:

> people are prepared to put up with verse from the lips of personages dressed in the fashion of some distant age; they should be made to hear it from people dressed like ourselves, living in houses and apartments like ours, and using telephones and motor cars and radio sets. (SP 79)

Fry on the other hand pragmatically superimposed imaginative and undisguised verse on a groundwork of behaviour conforming to the expectations of ordinary life (or fairly ordinary life, given that few people find themselves, for instance, threatened with burning either as a witch or in a duke's observatory). He claimed that there was in practice no problem:

> I do not believe that audiences as a whole disassociate themselves because the clothes on the characters on stage are different from the clothes on their backs, so long as thought and language are contemporary.

> Neither do I think the audiences have any difficulty in accepting poetry as the natural idiom of a play which is dressed and housed in the current fashion.[6]

Yeats and Eliot defended their need to write in verse by criticising the lack of power of prose, and this brings them to the difficulty of making a clear distinction between verse and prose. Eliot suggested a three-way division between verse, prose and ordinary unpolished conversation (with all its repetitions, hesitations and awkwardnesses). Indeed, he adds a fourth variety by dividing verse into the functional, unobtrusive verse dialogue – prose in metre, as it were – and genuine poetry when intensity of emotion is expressed in effective language. But it seems that even Eliot's four-fold division does no justice to the infinite variety of possible languages, most of them based on some convention which the audience, consciously or unconsciously, adjusts to. Eliot's starting point is not deciding which convention he is going to choose, but deciding which conventions depart not too noticeably from the imitation of everyday life. If he is not to use one of the many varieties of prose for this, then he has to use a prose-like verse. To this the convention of realism compels him.

Eliot's pursuit of conversational poetry then is perfectly logical if his basic assumptions are accepted. But Fry also imitated the ordinary life of various societies, some of them modern, without endorsing all Eliot's assumptions, and he made audiences listen to poetry spoken by people like themselves, which was Eliot's ambition. Fry, however, offered as his justification that in real life many people utter striking and poetic phrases. This may well be so, just as many people also in real life make jokes and witty remarks, but they do not use poetic phrases *all* the time, any more than they use nothing but the glittering repartee of Noel Coward.

Yeats too noted that modern educated and well-bred people 'have no artistic and charming language except light persiflage'.[7] He was perceptive in seeing that 'persiflage' is the one opportunity for the average person to make use of more than the normal potential of words, and to exploit his language for special effect. The unexpectedness and incongruities of meaning in verbal wit are essential to comic effect, but ordinary functional speech is not expected to attract this kind of attention. Both in verse and in literary prose, that is, carefully wrought prose with intentionally different layers of meaning, as in Ibsen or Pinter, attention is called to other than functional meaning, to a far greater extent than in casual utterance, or what Eliot called 'ordinary speech'. And indeed, both prose dialogue in poetic, patterned, metaphorical style, and the bald phrases selected from everyday discourse but given resonance from highlighting in a new context, make a dramatic language which can be called either 'poetic', or, less confusingly, 'literary', or 'creative'.

So, essentially, verse drama does not have a monopoly of poetic qualities: rather, its metre signals that it is putting more emphasis on the full exploitation of language, as well as having an intrinsic rhythmic effect. If, on the other hand, imitation of real life is a major objective, then the constraints spread from the language to the plot and characters and vice versa. Eliot discovered that 'the author is limited by the kind of poetry, and the degree of intensity in its kind, which can be plausibly attributed to each character in his play' (3VP 9–10). It is not clear whether he really means 'plausibly' in the sense of meeting some sort of realistic standards, or 'appropriately' within a given convention: for instance, the Women of Canterbury in *Murder in the Cathedral* express an appropriate community anguish as chorus, but whether their expression is plausible is a different matter.

Eliot was on firmer ground when he accepted convention:

> A verse play is not a play done into verse, but a different kind of play: in a way more realistic than 'naturalistic drama', because instead of clothing nature in poetry, it should remove the surface of things, expose the underneath or the inside of the natural surface appearance. It may allow the characters to behave inconsistently, but only with respect to a deeper consistency. It may use any device to show their real feelings and volitions, instead of just what, in actual life, they would normally profess or be conscious of; it must reveal, underneath the vacillating or infirm character, the indomitable unconscious will, and underneath the resolute purpose of the planning animal, the victim of circumstances and the doomed or sanctified being.[8]

Probably all the writers of poetic drama would agree with this manifesto, but ironically it was Eliot himself who was to deviate from it most.

Not many of the other poetic dramatists concerned themselves with realism as a consistent convention for their plays – the realistic prose dialogue of Auden's *The Ascent of F6* is only one element amid several non-realistic ones. Yeats declared that he was only happy writing 'when my people speak verse, or in words like those we put into verse' (V 712). Fry explained likewise that a poetic dramatist was bound to express the underlying feelings rather than normal banal utterance, and Auden said 'Dramatic speech should have the same confessed, significant, and undocumentary character, as dramatic movement'.[9] This statement comes from a series of formulations by Auden about drama, reminiscent of Brecht's dicta on the epic theatre round about 1930. Brecht was an early and systematic theorist of the non-illusionist theatre of the twentieth century, and what he says about this kind of theatre casts a clearer light on the poetic dramatists' narrower concern with the place of poetry. Brecht shared with Yeats, Auden and Isherwood and the early Eliot the view that theatrical performance is conventional, artificial and distinct from everyday life. These writers relegated psychological exploration to lesser importance than religious or social themes. Auden wrote: 'The drama is not suited to the analysis of character, which is the province of the novel. Dramatic characters are simplified, easily recognisable and over life-size'[10] (though *F6* seems to plunge into Freudian orthodoxy); Yeats thought that tragic character transcended the merely individual; Eliot considered all poetry as essentially impersonal rather than personal; and Brecht frequently labelled psychological study for its own sake as self-indulgent and distracting:

> In modern society the motions of the individual psyche are utterly uninteresting; it was only in feudal times that a king's or a leader's passions meant anything. Today they don't. Not even Hitler's personal passions; that's not what has brought Germany to her present condition, worse luck.[11]

Brecht places poetry amongst the other elements of non-illusionist theatre, recommending its presentation to the audience clearly *as* poetry. He wished to avoid carrying the audience off into an emotional orgy, where the effects would operate on them undistinguishably: a more lasting impact would result from presenting poetry, song, realistic dialogue or whatever to the audience separately.

> So let us invite all the sister arts of the drama, not in order to create an 'integrated work of art' in which they all offer themselves up and are lost, but so that together with the drama they may further the common task in their different ways; and their relations with one another consist in this: that they lead to mutual alienation.[12]

(Alienation means here detachment or 'making strange' to promote a conscious attention and reflection.)

Only Auden and Isherwood consistently made use of this mixture of 'different ways', and the crudely developed content of their plays did not supply the necessary unifying 'common task'. Eliot and Fry began by juxtaposing different effects, but moved towards an appearance of realism; Yeats, in spite of his liking for detached stylised acting and his separation of dance and chorus from dialogue, probably was aiming at an integrated experience for the audience. However, a later generation was to employ verse in the way Brecht described more successfully. Nowadays, plays using realistic situations with continuous verse dialogue in the Yeats–Eliot tradition are rare, and it is in the area of non-illusionist theatre, with a mixture of songs, music, verse and prose that the present and future use of dramatic poetry seems most productive.

2

Yeats and the Development of his Theory and Practice

> I think the theatre must be reformed in its plays, its speaking, its acting and its scenery. That is to say, I think there is nothing good about it at present. (E 107)

Over his long career, Yeats's plays developed as radically as did his other poetry. His earlier, lyrical or *folklorique* plays are now mainly played by amateur and school companies, and the later more enigmatic Noh and Dance plays attract student productions in university drama departments and drama schools, but on the whole the London professional theatre has not shown any interest in reviving Yeats's work. Nonetheless it seems likely that it is only a matter of time before the important plays from each stage of his career find their place in the repertoire of the serious subsidised companies. The obvious candidates for revival among the earlier plays are *Countess Cathleen*, *Cathleen Ni Houlihan* and *Deirdre*, all of which have the powerful, wistful Irish charm so often satirised in Irish comedies, but none the less valid for that. Several of the Cuchulain plays, such as *On Baile's Strand*, *At the Hawk's Well* and *The Only Jealousy of Emer* have a gripping tragic irony; and the Open University television production of *Purgatory* demonstrated its continuing dramatic power; Yeats's late *The Words upon the Windowpane* and *Purgatory*, complete but short plays, would make a compulsive if harrowing double bill.

Yeats commented 'I had three interests: interest in a form of literature, in a form of philosophy, and belief in nationality. None of these seemed to have anything to do with the other' (E 263). Early influences may have sharpened this awareness of conflicting values: born in Ireland in 1865, he spent long periods in England when his artist father moved the family there in pursuit of patronage, but these periods were interrupted by long holidays with Irish relatives, and Yeats chose to attend a Dublin art college. Both his English schooling and the London literary circle in which he mixed even as an impoverished and unproved young poet, made him the more aware of what it was to be Irish, and unlike Shaw and Wilde, and later Joyce, all of whom he knew quite well, Yeats continued to give both his presence and his slightly exasperated loyalty to Ireland.

The influences on his career came from surprisingly different directions. More influential than anything else was his meeting with the young Irish political activist, Maud Gonne, in 1888. He seems to have fallen instantly and permanently in love with her striking beauty, and in spite of recurrent disillusion and frustration, his obsession with her – her beauty, her personality, her friendly implacable rejection of him as a lover – is evident to the end of his life. Maude Gonne was a campaigner for Irish independence, and in her company Yeats attended political meetings and demonstrations. For her he wrote

Countess Cathleen, hoping she would play the title role, and she did in fact play Cathleen ni Houlihan in his play of that name. Yet his own interest was primarily in the quality of life, the experience of Irish culture, rather than what he saw as the degrading and superficial manoeuvrings of practical politics, and he seems to have had an underlying hope that he could live up to Maud Gonne's nationalism by cultural rather than violent activities.

The other main influence in Yeats's life was Lady Gregory, whom he met through Edward Martyn, a minor Irish literary acquaintance. Lady Gregory, widow of a landowner, would have been congenial in the first place for sharing Yeats's interest in Irish cultural traditions, as she was a collector of oral folk material from her tenants, but unexpectedly she responded to his theatrical interest:

> We sat there through the wet afternoon, and though I had never been at all interested in theatres our talk turned on plays. Mr. Martyn had written two . . . I said it was a pity we had no Irish theatre where such plays could be given. Mr. Yeats said that had always been a dream of his, but he had of late thought it an impossible one, for it could not at first pay its way, and there was no money to be found for such a thing in Ireland. We went on talking about it, and things seemed to grow possible as we talked, and before the end of the afternoon we had made our plan. We said we would collect money, or rather ask to have a certain sum of money guaranteed. We would then take a Dublin theatre and give a performance of Mr. Martyn's *Heather Field* and one of Mr. Yeats's own plays, *The Countess Cathleen*. I offered the first guarantee of £25.[1]

This historic meeting took place in 1897 and Yeats added

that 'our first players came from England, but presently we began our real work with a company of Irish amateurs'. During its first few years the Irish Literary Theatre, as the movement called itself, camped out in various local halls and meeting rooms, more or less suitable, as George Moore the novelist described:

> A lofty hall with a balcony and benches down the middle, and there were seats along the walls placed so that those who sat in them would have to turn their heads to see the stage, a stage that had been constructed hurriedly by advancing some rudely painted wings and improvising a drop curtain.[2]

Then in 1904 Miss Annie Horniman, an Englishwoman with money of her own, who had designed and made costumes for some of the early plays, offered to have the Mechanics Institute theatre and ajoining City Morgue in Abbey Street converted and brought up to professional standards at her own expense for Yeats's company to rent: this was the beginning of the famous Abbey Theatre, Dublin.

Throughout his life, in fact, Yeats was deeply involved with the development of the Irish National Theatre Movement; he believed this was the main reason for his getting the Nobel Prize for Literature in 1922. The practical experience that his close involvement with theatre brought him meant that he had a solid basis from which to say to audiences 'Not what you want but what we want': he was able to make his own mistakes. But as he commented in retrospect in 1919 'We set out to make a "People's Theatre", and in that we have succeeded' except that, paradoxically 'we did not set out to create this sort of theatre' (E 244): this people's theatre turned out to be not quite what he meant at all, because it was, as the Abbey manifested it, sincere, moving, truthful, but not poetic. In a period of theatrical falsity, the truthfulness was a major achievement, but where his fellow workers aimed at the truthfulness of realism, Yeats's priority was the truthfulness to spiritual experience.

The Land of Heart's Desire (1894) foreshadowed the later plays in having its dancing representative of the supernatural world, here in the role of the fairy child, written for the niece of the actress, Florence Farr. The fairy child lures the discontented young wife, Mary Bruin, from the house of her materialistic father-in-law, grumbling mother-in-law and adoring but unimaginative husband Shawn. All are fascinated by the beautiful child, even the priest, Father Hart, who takes down the crucifix because it frightens her. Mary like so many of Yeats's characters is torn between this world and another, between dull reliable happiness and the thoughtless joy of the inhuman world. The conflict is presented in simple domestic terms, but it is presented fairly and even with ambiguity: in spite of its dullness, the 'excellent old way of love' must be a good thing, and 'maddening freedom and bewildering light' outside God's peace may or may not be a good thing. Mary dies at the height of the child's persuasion, but her last words are the indecisive 'and yet . . .'.

At this point Yeats was writing in blank verse, in spite of misgivings about its 'Renaissance' associations, but although he allowed some imitation Shakespeare to creep into the dialogue – Shawn wishes to 'crowd the enraptured quiet of the sky / With candles burning to your lonely face' (V 193) – it is rather the echoes of Pater which lend a long dying cadence to the verse. Much of this characteristic vague, indefinite, non-assertive vocabulary, 'pale', 'dawn', 'dreams', 'moon', as in 'her face is pale as water before dawn', was later excised by Yeats as 'mere ornament', and he came to prefer it with 'all needless and all mere lyrical passages cut away' (V 212).

'Amateurs perform it more often than any other play of mine' (V 212) Yeats noted – its simplicity, strong character types, and nice role for the precocious child actress no doubt making it attractive. With these 'first experiments on blank verse' Yeats recommended keeping 'all the players except the fairy child as still and statuesque as possible, so that the blank verse where there is so little animation seemed their natural utterance' (V 212). He was not here merely aiming for a 'simple and natural' effect from his amateur players, but seeking a new style. Working with amateurs, Yeats was free to experiment with ideas on acting, sets, costume and music as well as with the content of his plays, without being hampered by commercial pressures or professional shibboleths.

One experiment was designed to make the speaking of dramatic verse more musical: verse should go out of its way to proclaim itself verse, and never try to pretend to be realistic conversation. Therefore with the actress Florence Farr he invented a means of speaking to a limited number of notes struck as accompaniment on a psaltery especially made for her by Arnold Dolmetsch. In 'Speaking to the Psaltery'[3] the scores of suggested settings are given, but the effect was not up to Yeats's hopes. Joseph Holloway, the Dublin architect and invaluable diarist of theatrical events, commented:

> This lilting, or what you will, to notes, though made quite pleasing and beautiful by Miss Farr for short periods . . . would, I imagine, become very trying if continued for any length of time, even by an artist like

> Miss Farr. What then would it be in a tyro's charge? Monotonous agony from which Lord deliver us! (JH 19)

Yeats was defensive about his experiments, because, as was well known, he himself was virtually tone deaf, which may explain the failure of the innovation: George Moore exclaimed 'Lord save us! Quarter tones! Why, he can't tell a high note from a low one'.[4] But his continuing wish to differentiate and as it were 'frame' the poetry of his plays probably attracted him later to the Noh form with its percussion and string accompaniments to the choruses, and he was able to try the dramatic effect of intoned delivery in two full length plays before abandoning it.

The theme of *The Countess Cathleen* (1882) is one of saintly self-sacrifice, as Countess Cathleen finds that the peasants are selling their souls to two demons for money and food during a famine. She bargains to redeem them all by selling her own pure and much more precious soul. Against the pleas of her old nurse and the young bard Aleel, this transaction is carried out.

Cathleen is unable to survive without her soul, and dies, but because of her goodness, she is received into heaven and the demons are cheated of their prey. Like the removal of the crucifix in *The Land of Heart's Desire* this buying and selling of souls caused an uproar among audiences. The play was the inaugural production of the Irish Literary Theatre and the controversy was prophetic of its stormy history. Yeats was assailed by the theological points that souls cannot be used as currency in this way, and even if they were, Cathleen should not then be redeemed after all, her sale nullified by her good motive. In addition, the patriotic objection was raised that Irish peasants could never be so forgetful of their religion.

Yeats's own lack of religious commitment had made him underestimate the effect on the Irish audience, and he admitted: 'In using what I considered traditional symbols I forgot that in Ireland they are not symbols but realities'.[5] For his purposes it had seemed an orthodox deployment of his themes. Materialism, this worldliness, is paradoxically offered by two other-worldly demons, while Cathleen is willing to die to prove the value of the spirit – again paradoxically to lose her soul to prove its worth. There is an unambiguous confrontation between good and evil, but a more complex element is added by the role of the bard Aleel, who tries to persuade Cathleen to a third option, to abandon both peasants and comfortable resignation for the forgetfulness and immortality of the pagan fairy world. He fails, and loses his last hopes of her love.

Again Yeats continued his simplifying of his blank verse style, purging away self-conscious poeticisms, such as the peasant woman's inappropriately Shakespearian 'Gilding your tongue with the calamitous times' (V 10). Yeats was not interested in the supposed similarity of blank verse to natural speech rhythms. It was the *difference* of blank verse, as of all verse rhythms, from prose style that he wished to stress. He argued that poetic language was a convention which should not be camouflaged in realistic settings (which would in any case only produce an effect of incongruity) but should be complemented by other non-realistic stage conventions. In *The Countess Cathleen* the scene in the wood is suggested 'all in flat colour, without light and shade and against a diapered or gold back ground'; the castle hall is tapestried, and Yeats later called the play 'a tapestry'.

In performance, the sum of these ideas produced a

mixed impression: Joseph Holloway found the play 'weirdly, fantastically, pathetically, or picturesquely effective by turns', but added

> Note. Chanting is hard to follow until the ear grows accustomed to listening to measured rhythm. Many of the artists failed to allow those in front to clearly understand what they spoke. This should not be, of course, as the first essential of effective stage work is the clearness of articulation in the speech of the actors. (JH 8)

Both Yeats and Eliot had the problem of realising on stage the spiritual or supernatural aspect of their themes, and their ideas were ahead of their time, or hopelessly impractical, according to one's point of view. Yeats had wanted *Cathleen* to end with a stunning transformation scene set on a mountain slopc whcrc 'half in light, half in the shadow stand armed angels. . . . They stand as if upon the air in formation of battle and look downward with stern faces.' As one might expect, at the Abbey Theatre 'a shallow stage made the elaborate vision of armed angels upon a mountainside impossible' (V 173). Later technology and the use of projection or film would have put this effect within the scope of a cramped theatre, but Yeats had to substitute one angel, passing 'with eyes fixed' from stage left to stage right. The stage picture then is reminiscent of mediaeval miniature: Yeats's production created its 'weird' and 'picturesque' effect through static tableaux, two-dimensional sets and chanted dialogue, and the scale remained small. The number of angels is in any case irrelevant to the method of staging: how 'realistic' should the angel be?

The same problem appears in *The Shadowy Waters*

(1911). Here the hero king Forgael is sailing to seek happiness beyond the edge of the world, following the souls of the departed which appear to him as man-headed birds. Neither the treachery of his sailors nor the reasonings of his sceptical friend Aibric can turn him back, even when they capture a wealthy ship, kill its passenger king and capture the beautiful queen Dectora. Another magical element is Forgael's harp, with which he subdues the mutineers and enchants Dectora into the belief that she is in love with him. The conclusion shows the influence of Villiers de l'Isle Adam's quest play *Axel*, in that Forgael, even having found the perfect love, cannot resist going on following the 'ash-grey birds', so that, deserted by the others, he and Dectora continue sailing alone on what has become a quest for the sake of questing.

It seems that Yeats hoped to fill the stage with these magical spirits in bodily manifestation, as he is said to have told a dismayed Lady Gregory that half the characters had eagles' faces, but he settled eventually for a more effective ambiguity. Only Forgael ever sees the man-headed birds, so his quest may be a true one, or a delusion of the spirits, or a self-delusion in Forgael's mind.

On the other hand, the magic harp must appear on stage and is required to burn with a supernatural light when in use. Yeats describes the practical problems:

> the stage carpenter found it very difficult to make the crescent shaped harp that was to burn with fire; and besides, no matter how well he made the frame, there was no way of making the strings take fire. I had therefore, to give up the harp for a sort of psaltery, a little like the psaltery Miss Farr speaks to, where the

> strings could be slits covered with glass or gelatine on the surface of a shallow and perhaps semitransparent box. (V 341)

He added 'There is no reason for objecting to a mechanical effect when it represents some material thing, becomes a symbol, a player, as it were' and the defensive tone suggests that the effect was not universally praised. Like Eliot, Yeats was dissatisfied with the staging of supernatural forces, but instead of eliminating them as Eliot did, he was to seek the solution in a dramatic convention.

Yeats's ideas on the visual presentation of his plays, apart from the magical equipment, is soundly based on acceptance of convention. He rejects 'flashy landscape painting' on backcloths, in order to be consistent with the obviously non-naturalistic verse dialogue: 'we can only get rid of the sense of unreality that most of us feel when we listen to the conventional speech of Shakespeare, by making the scenery as conventional'.[6] In *The Shadowy Waters* he worked out the principle of having two main colours for the background and costumes, with contrasting touches of a third – here dark blue and green with some copper. The first production was again at its best harmoniously evocative of a refined beauty and aspiration in the audience, and at its worst inaudible and baffling. Joseph Holloway's description suggests consistency of pace, tone and movement carried to extremes of monotony, and an audience which, as at a religious festival, endured for the sake of proving cultural superiority rather than for dramatic reasons:

> W. B. Yeats's weird, puzzling, melancholy, and depressingly gloomy dramatic poem, *The Shadowy*

> *Waters* . . . fairly mystified the audience by the uncanny monotony of its strange incomprehensibleness, until a peculiar not wholly disagreeable dreariness filled the minds of all who listened to the strange music of the chanted words . . . personally I am very pleased to have witnessed the experiment of presenting it on the stage. It was strangely tiresome but very beautiful and lovely all the same. (JH 32)

And later Yeats was to say 'At first I was driven into teaching too statuesque a pose, too monotonous a delivery' (V 1299).

Yeats's next few plays were of a different kind: written in collaboration with Lady Gregory, they were fairly realistic in setting and vigorous in action. *Where There is Nothing* (1902) and its rewriting as *The Unicorn from the Stars* (1907) are both picaresque works: their protagonists both have visions and trances which lead them to embark on a career of Bacchic destruction aided by outcasts such as tinkers and beggars, and both finally realise they should have been transforming themselves rather than attacking external social forms. The message was less clear than this summary implies, and *The Unicorn* was greeted with 'laughter in the wrong places' (JH 96). But *Cathleen Ni Houlihan* (1902) which shares the theme of the call of the ideal and the problem of balancing humour and seriousness, was immediately successful, and is still one of Yeats's best known plays. Cathleen is the personification in the shape of an old woman of the claims of Ireland. She intrudes on a peasant family very similar to that in *The Land of Heart's Desire* where the son Michael is about to marry a pretty girl with a good dowry, and so inspires him with self-forgetful patriotism that when the cry goes up that a French force is landing to aid an Irish uprising against the English occupiers, Michael rushes out to join the rebellion.

The play appeals first by its establishment of the peasant's way of life: the details of cottage life, the kindliness to strangers alongside keen attention to money matters. The Old Woman (Cathleen) laments that her troubles began when she lost 'My four beautiful green fields' (the four counties of Ireland), and the peasant couple promptly try to identify her as a neighbour:

> PETER (*aside to Bridget*): Do you think could she be the widow Casey that was put out of her holding at Kilglass a while ago?
>
> BRIDGET: She is not. I saw the widow Casey one time at the market in Ballina, a stout fresh woman. (V 223)

This seems to be Lady Gregory's dialogue, but some of the more poetic, 'weird' passages sound like Yeats, as for instance in the Old Woman's best known speech:

> It is hard service they take that help me. Many that are red-cheeked now will be pale-cheeked; many that have been free to walk the hills and the bogs and the rushes will be sent to walk hard streets in far countries; many a good plan will be broken; many that have gathered money will not stay to spend it; many a child will be born and there will be no father at its christening to give it a name. They that have red cheeks will have pale cheeks for my sake, and for all that, they will think they are well paid.
>
> (*She goes out; her voice is heard outside singing.*)
>
> They shall be remembered for ever,
> They shall be alive for ever,
> They shall be speaking for ever,
> The people shall hear them for ever. (V 229)

Yeats, however, was not quite sure whether the two styles had balanced as well as Holloway thought: 'the mild humour of the part before Kathleen [sic] came in kept the house in such delighted laughter, that it took them some little while to realise the tragic meaning of Kathleen's part' (L 368). The plot was based on a dream Yeats had, and the songs or verse speeches were sung to a tune supposedly heard in a dream by an actor. These songs show Yeats's liking for adding another dimension by a more concentrated lyrical form, here as in his verse plays.

Although this is one of the more realistic plays, 'the first of our Irish School of folk-drama' which he later left others to write, the concept of Cathleen as symbol is in line with his preference for mythic, universally significant material. *A Pot of Broth* (1904) on the other hand, is a light piece, well known to amateurs, being the story of a tramp who convinces a peasant couple that by boiling a 'magic' stone in plain water he can produce broth, which in fact is achieved by his unobtrusively adding all the usual ingredients (chicken, ham, meal) filched from the kitchen. As Yeats says, its theme is 'rather imitative', though he may have felt some sympathy for the adventurer who makes something out of nothing through his personality and persuasive language.

About *Cathleen Ni Houlihan* Yeats wrote 'My play, "The Land of Heart's Desire" was in a sense, the call of the heart, the heart seeking its own dream: this play is the call of country, and I have a plan of following it up with a little play about the call of religion' (V 235). This last has been identified tentatively with *The Hour Glass*, its prose version written in 1903. Here a Wise Man, who has convinced the whole country that 'there is nothing we cannot see; there is nothing we cannot touch' (V 626) is himself forcibly convinced otherwise by the appearance of an Angel, who gives him an hour, by the hour glass, to live, and moreover condemns him to hell unless within that time he can find one person who still believes in God.

As in the other 'call' plays, then, a visitant from another world attacks the materialism of the mortal protagonist, but here as in *Countess Cathleen* the choice is an absolute one; the Wise Men cannot really choose materialism which is its own punishment because the Angel's call is backed up by the sanction of eternal punishment in hell. In conclusion, the Wise Man, failing to reconvert pupils, wife or children, turns in terror to the Fool. The Fool is too cautious to commit himself, but when the Wise Man kneels to him, in the earlier prose version the Fool testifies and the Wise Man is saved. Yeats disliked this ending:

> An action on the stage, however, is so much stronger than a word that when the Wise Man abused himself before the Fool I was always ashamed . . . last year I changed action and all. I made a new play of it, and when I had finished discovered how I might have taken the offence out of the old by a change of action so slight that a reader would hardly have noticed it. (V 646)

This change is to make the Fool keep refusing to admit his faith, so that the Wise Man rises again, and proves his true and disinterested conversion by accepting God's will:

> Be silent. May God's will prevail on the instant,
> Though His will be my eternal pain. (V 637)

Yeats's idea of rejecting the material world for the spiritual had at first come too close to rejecting wisdom and elevating gross ignorance, 'as do ignorant preachers'. The Wise Man's final reliance on God's will is a more profound choice, and is not unlike Becket's in *Murder in the Cathedral*.

Yeats had remarked that 'my words flow freely alone when my people speak in verse, or in words like those we put into verse' (V 712). By implying equivalence here, he seems to be obliterating the distinction between verse and prose, but he found it worthwhile in 1914 to write a verse arrangement of the prose original. Though both versions sustain concentrated meanings and, being formal, include patterned structure and imagery, the verse compresses the flowing conversational Irish speech into a more clipped shape, and thus 'O that the grass and plants could speak! Somebody has said that they would wither if they doubted. O, speak to me, O glass-blades. O fingers of God's certainty, speak to me. You are millions and you will not speak!' becomes

> The sap would die out of the blades of grass
> Had they a doubt. They understand it all,
> Being the fingers of God's certainty,
> Yet can but make their sign into the air. (V 629)

The first production was designed according to Yeats's 'three colour principle' in front of an olive-green curtain with Wise Man and pupils in shades of purple and the Fool in red-brown, with an effective set designed by T. Sturge Moore, very square and symmetrical to suggest the Wise Man's rigid materialistic frame of mind. The Angel was not humanised, but appeared with a gold-covered face as in mediaeval pictures and dramas, which powerfully suggests the superhuman behind the superfically human, as does a mask. The impact of the spiritual upon complacent humanity impressed audiences greatly: 'it was only too effective, converting a music-hall singer and sending him to Mass for six weeks' (V 645).

The simple, folklorique episodic story, in which the series of exchanges with pupils, wife, children and fool build up to a climax is used again in a more extended serial plot in *The King's Threshold* (1904). It is a classic structure, imposed upon Greek tragedy by the limited number of actors, found in English in Milton's *Samson Agonistes*, and soon to appear in *Murder in the Cathedral*. The plot of *The King's Threshold* is carefully built up, as a series of tempters come to persuade the hero Seanachan to give up his hunger strike on the king Guaire's threshold. He refuses; he is a poet who has had his traditional place at the king's council taken away, and insists that he will die unless the insult to poetry is withdrawn. The offers of food, the appeals of the Mayor that his townsfolk will be victimised, the pleas of his pupils, the princesses, and his sweetheart Fedelm are all refused, and it becomes increasingly certain that the play can only end with Seanachan's death or victory. This simple plot is given depth by the king's dilemma; like Creon in *Antigone*, he puts a persuasive rationale of his decree – the council after all is for decision-makers, not artists, his pragmatism shading into the justification that 'might is right'. But to Seanachan his place at the council is a recognition of the value of poetry. Guaire, like Conchubar in the later *Deirdre*, is trapped in his own role as king and cannot step down from his dignity and avoid disaster – for the death of a poet on the threshold will bring appalling bad luck as well as popular disaffection – by revoking his decision.

Yeats had originally intended to end the play tragically, and though he temporarily heeded a friend who pleaded for 'a few happy moments in the Theatre', he made the tragic version the final one, so that Seanachan dies, after Fedelm and his pupils think better of their efforts to make him live and instead urge him to die for the honour of poetry. The celebration of Seanachan's victory in death is spoken by his pupils, but earlier commentary on the action has been made by two cripples who have a choral function in adding the outsider's viewpoint. They contribute to the comic relief of the Mayor's scenes, which Synge thought to be a mistake, but their comments are, in spite of their cunning self-interest, surprisingly sympathetic, and they seem to be an early version of the masterly use Yeats makes of Blind Man and Fool as chorus and subplot in *On Baile's Strand*.

The musicians in *Deirdre* (1907) approximate much nearer to the traditional chorus; they are three travelling women musicians who arrive at the guest lodge just before Deirdre and her lover Naoise, and are present throughout the action without taking much active part in it, and give relevant but not obvious comment in their songs. After years of exile, Deirdre and Naoise have been invited to return for reconciliation by King Conchubar, from whom they eloped together on the eve of his marriage to Deirdre. Synge, in his play on the subject, had motivated their return by showing Deirdre as anxious to force a crisis, fearing the effect of change and age – of time, in short – on their once perfect but human love. Yeats's lovers are more naïve, but also hint at dissatisfaction with endless freedom. His Deirdre fears a trap from the first. A major factor is Naoise's adherence to the standards of a heroic tradition:

Being High King, he cannot break his faith.
I have his word and I must take that word,
Or prove myself unworthy of my nurture
Under a great man's roof. (V 355)

Unfortunately Conchubar's idea of the behaviour of a High King is different and his messenger reveals that Deirdre can only buy Naoise's life by willingly becoming Conchubar's bride: this will wipe out the ridicule inflicted on him by their elopement. Again Naoise accepts his role and is killed defending Deirdre against all the odds. Yeats's Deirdre is a vital, resourceful character: she tries in many ways to force events to her will. She tries role-playing to persuade Naoise to leave before it is too late, by pretending some interest in Conchubar to rouse his jealousy; similarly when Naoise is dead she pretends a pragmatic acceptance of the *fait accompli*, to induce the suspicious Conchubar to let her lay out her dead lover, when she really intends to kill herself on his body.

Yeats's choice of emphasis within the given story outline means that we see the actual process of the free person accepting destiny, the individual assuming the mask. There is a certain inevitability about the fates of Deirdre and Naoise, given Conchubar's implacability and the overwhelming odds, but also there is an element of choice in the type of mask chosen, or in the way of assuming it. Yeats's Deirdre, although she may not have the superficial traits of a comedy character, is nonetheless not so universal as to be without character, as may be seen by comparing her with the quite different Deirdre of Synge. Moreover Synge's play was in prose, and although his prose is colourful and evocative enough to have all the qualities of poetry except regular rhythm, it is rhythm which gives Yeats's verse that added conclusiveness or absoluteness that fits his tragic vision. Both would like to follow the model of another trapped king and queen, and die with dignity, playing chess:

> What need have I, that gave up all for love,
> To die like an old king out of a fable,
> Fighting and passionate? What need is there
> For all that ostentation at my setting?
> I have loved truly and betrayed no man,
> I need no lightning at the end, no beating
> In a vain fury at the cage's door. (V 374)

Naoise weighs different kinds of reaction, reflected in the weak rhythm of the rapid 'Fighting and passionate . . . my setting . . . no beating', as against the conclusive monosyllables rounding off his self-justification: 'all for love . . . betrayed no man'. In the event, he cannot remain passive, however dignified, and rushes out to die heroically and uselessly. As well as the impact of the repeated 'I' and Yeats's favourite bird imagery, the framing effect of the verse form impresses the universal significance of Naoise's dilemma – acceptance or defiance – more immediately upon the audience.

Deirdre is a powerful play and offers a tempting role for an actress: Yeats showed some lack of faith in his company by importing the professional actress, Miss Darragh, which caused ill-feeling in the company and predictably conflicted with the new style he was supposed to be promoting. Frank Fay said:

> It was like putting a Rolls Royce to run a race with a lot of hill ponies up the mountains of Morne, bogs and all. . . . On the one hand Miss Darragh made our company look young and simple, and on the other

> hand their youth and simplicity made her look as if she were overacting.[7]

Joseph Holloway at first liked her 'consistent and beautiful' Deirdre, though it 'had too much of the flesh and too little of the *spirituelle* in its composition' (JH 75) but on a second visit thought her interpretation 'does not improve on acquaintance; it lacks sincerity and charm' (JH 77); however, the even more professional Mrs Patrick Campbell later triumphed over these problems when her long acquaintanceship with Yeats and her eye for a good part brought her to the Abbey: she 'fitted in perfectly with her surroundings, and a perfectly harmonious whole resulted. She is too great an artist to let herself get outside the picture for a moment.' The great actress had quite enough power to fill the role:

> Her cajoling 'Concobar' into allowing her to attend to the dead body of her beloved 'Naisi' was a supreme piece of dramatic art, full of subtlety and intense emotionalism. Her savage outburst on his refusing her first request was superb in its tigerish savagery; the baffled women let loose the floodgates of her wrath on the loveless old man who had waded through crime to attain her, and annihilated him into submission.
>
> (JH 120)

Yeats's mature period begins with his next pre-Noh tragedy, *On Baile's Strand* (1904), which moves to the saga of his main hero, Cuchulain. This play has the archetypal theme of the father who unknowingly kills his own son. Cuchulain's enemy, the warrior queen Aoife, has conceived this child in a mid-battle encounter and, unknown to him, brought up the boy to kill Cuchulain in revenge for her former defeat, embittered by his desertion of her. Presentiment of natural feeling makes Cuchulain love the young stranger, but the High King Conchubar orders them to fight. Cuchulain kills the boy, learns of his true identity, and rushes out, maddened, to fight the waves of the sea.

The plot is tightly organised, opening as the lesser kings gather to give a new oath of absolute obedience to Conchubar, to defend a new age of stability. Cuchulain alone is unwilling to be bound, but agrees in bitterness when all his heroic warriors urge him to it, reproaching them:

> It's you that have changed. You've wives and children
> now,
> And for that reason cannot follow one
> That lives like a bird's flight from tree to tree. (V 493)

Here, as when he mocks Conchubar for building a timid security for his weak children, Cuchulain's unspoken sensitivity to his own childlessness (as he thinks) is ironically apparent, and the oath he instinctively resents forces him against his instincts to fight his own son. The oath also shows Cuchulain giving up his old irresponsibility to become one who fulfils a role – superficially, that of Conchubar's champion, but at a deeper level, that of the fate-doomed father who kills his child. At a deeper level still, his preference for freedom and the wandering life has perhaps been a self-absorbed state that avoids commitment, here personified by the desired but destroyed child.

Like *Deirdre* the stage picture is given an extra framework by its choral figures, the Blind Man and the

Fool. They are unheroic, squabbling petty thieves, and practically they set the action in context and finally reveal the identity of his dead son to Cuchulain. Symbolically they reflect in parodic form the relationship of Conchubar and Cuchulain: the Blind Man's wisdom is limited by his blindness, as is Conchubar by his pragmatic materialism; and the Fool's active recklessness and liability to be distracted by the imaginative loses him his share of their thefts, just as Cuchulain throws caution aside to make the disastrous heroic gesture. The Fool's description of Cuchulain's concluding off-stage warring with the ocean seems a verbal equivalent of the dance in the dance plays (one version of the 'sequel' play in the cyle, *Fighting the Waves*, was preceded by a ballet presenting this struggle). Thus, the elements of Noh style are already present in fragmented form or suggestion, ready to be reassembled.

Cuchulain appears once more before the Noh influence begins to dominate, however, in the comic folk play *The Green Helmet* (1910). This is in 'ballad metre' which brings energy by its bounding rhythm to the quarrels of the three kings, Cuchulain, Conall and Laegaire, and the often clever rhymes reinforce the comedy. Cuchulain learns that supernatural Red Man has played the 'beheading game' with his fellow kings a year ago, and in this play Cuchulain is a clever folk hero – he forces reason and compromise on the other characters but, by freely offering his own head to the Red Man, proves his cunning is not cowardice, and is then crowned champion of Ireland.

Visually this production concluded what one might call Yeats's colourist period, and also suggests the danger for the poet of proposing imaginative conceptions which sound fascinating on paper, but do not work out in practical theatrical terms. The directions for the set read:

> the house is orange-red and the chairs and tables and flagons black with a slight purple tinge which is not clearly distinguishable from the black. The rocks are black with a few green touches. The sea is green and luminous, and all the characters except the Red Man and the Black Men are dressed in various shades of green, one or two with touches of purple. . . . The Red Man is altogether in red. He is tall, and his height increased by horns on the Green Helmet. The effect is intentionally violent and startling. (V 421)

and Yeats added in a note

> I have noticed that the more obviously decorative is the scene and costuming of any play, the more it is lifted out of time and place and the nearer to faeryland do we carry it. One also gets much more effect out of concerted movements – above all, if there are many players – when all the clothes are the same colour. (V 454)

Joseph Holloway liked the play, but thought that the 'talkative group of men and women who filled the stage was confused and unpicturesquely disposed. The dressing of the stage was sadly needed again' (JH 107). The conception was fine, but the execution seemed to lack effectiveness: Yeats's use of colour in large bold areas, aiming to avoid distraction from the playing, had to be carried out mainly by the use of dyed curtains, which can easily look limp and tawdry after too much manipulation. In 1901 he had admired Gordon Craig's 'severe, beautiful, simple effects of colour, that leave the imagination free to follow all the suggestions of the play' (L 366). Craig's development of all-purpose stage scenery in the form of his 'screens' seemed to solve the problem of using blocks of colour with pristine professionalism. These screens were a longer or shorter series of tall panels, double-hinged together, the panels being of various widths from one foot to several feet. They could be folded back and forth to make square pillars, walls with alcoves, angled corners, or gradually sloping near-curves.

These were adopted enthusiastically by Yeats, and in his note on *The Hour Glass* he charts his change from the three-colour principle to the blocks-of-light principle:

> Last winter, however, we revived the play with costumes taken chiefly from designs by Mr. Gordon Craig, and with the screens he has shown us how to make and use, arranged as in the drawing in this book, and with effects that depend but little on colour, and greatly upon delicate changes of tone. (V 644)

What Craig added to Yeats's colour sense was perhaps the feeling of 'wandering on the edge of eternity'[8] appropriate for a writer who wanted to introduce a spiritual, eternal dimension into his characters' lives. Practically, this meant, for instance, the changing of T. Sturge Moore's effective set for *The Hour Glass* for an asymmetrical set, where a series of screens, gradually angled to form a long curving wall, led from the Wise Man's desk round to an unknown depth, which he is forced eventually to confront. The desk is shown in shadow, and light issues from the unseen area. Craig made many of his best effects by light rather than colour, indeed he was accused of using too much chiaroscuro for its own sake, especially by actresses who did not like being left in the 'oscuro' areas, and Yeats found that getting rid of some of the clutter of scenery in wings and flies made lighting more flexible.

In practice, the screens were used mainly for Yeats's own plays and such fantasies as Lady Gregory's *The Dragon*; evidently the more realistic plays were felt to need realistic staging. Moreover, Craig licensed his screens to be used only at the Abbey proper, not on the necessary money-making tours, so though the screens remained exclusive (and undamaged), they never gained wide recognition outside a fairly limited audience. Holloway was hostile beforehand

> saw the stagehands setting Gordon Craig's new ideas of scenery – a series of square box-like pillars saffron-hued, with saffron background, wings, sky pieces and everything. The entire setting struck me, as like as peas, only on a big scale, of the blocks I as a child built houses of. As Yeats never played with blocks in his youth, Gordon Craig's childish ideas give him keen delight now. (JH 146)

and on the opening night reported that 'the Gordon Craig freak scenery and lighting' were considered 'an affected failure'.

The Player Queen (1922), begun as a tragedy in 1907, closes Yeats's Craig phase, and he attributes its non-Irishness to the cosmopolitan nature of the screens. The eponymous heroine is Decima, lead actress in a company of strolling players, who is proud of her dominance over her drunken poet husband Septimus, until she finds he has been deceiving her with the homely Nona; wounded in her self-esteem, she contemplates suicide but is interrupted by the real queen, fleeing from her first sight of her subjects, who have turned against her because of her reclusive habits. Decima successfully takes on the role of the queen (who retires to a convent) marries the prime minister, and exiles the strolling players. 'Its strange story baffled me', confessed Holloway, and this has been the reaction of subsequent critics. It has obvious coincidences with Genet's *The Balcony*, but without savagery or political background, and does not say very much about role-playing, though the opportunity is there. As in the preceding play Yeats seemed here happy to have large numbers of people moving about the stage, but practical considerations, such as the limited popularity of his plays, and the financial problems now that Miss Horniman had withdrawn her subsidy, were added to the aesthetic attractions of the pared down Noh form to which he turned next.

3
Later Yeats: the Noh Plays and After

Anyone who has seen the formal and alien effect of a Noh company performing the plays will realise that the text alone could have conveyed little of this effect to Yeats, and the compiler Fenollosa's notes on the salient points of performance can hardly have recreated the image and atmosphere for him. However, this is not ultimately relevant to what Yeats was doing: he was not after all a Japanese scholar aiming for an authentic reconstruction or imitation of the Noh models, but wished to make use of its conventions for his own purposes. His notes betray also a desire to get as far as possible from the commonplace limitations of the folk play:

> I have found my first model – and in literature if we would not be parvenues we must have a model – in the 'Noh' stage of aristocratic Japan. (V 415)

These words hint at the problems of inventing new forms in isolation out of thin air – better transform an old model than concoct arbitrary and flimsy rituals. An example of arbitrariness even within the borrowed tradition is the ritual of folding and unfolding the cloth which Yeats invented and added to the Noh model. Here a large piece of cloth is spread out by the chorus while a song is sung, then folded again. The actors can take up position behind the cloth, without needing a curtain. But having dispensed with illusion, there seems no reason why the actors should not enter in full view, as in Noh (or Greek) theatre; if painted backcloths are distracting, surely a billowing cloth is more so. (Later Yeats sometimes made the cloth optional, or omitted it.)

Richard Taylor's summary of Noh features suggests both what Yeats selected and what he left out from his model:

> The play is always based on a familiar incident closely associated with a famous place, and it is performed by a single character with only the most essential dramatic foils. The action itself is kept at a distance by avoiding realistic imitation. The focus of interest is the quality of experience involved, not the actual event, and the central incident is presented through various levels of recollection, dream, and vision, as well as aesthetic stylization. The text is often more poetic than dramatic in its dependence on patterns of imagery and connotations of literary and historical allusion.[1]

The acting, gestures and movement 'approach the condition of dance' in a way that perhaps could be compared with the symbolic gestures of classical ballet, and there are often two set dances evoking the central incident:

> The set dances are equally anti-realistic and either demonstrate a lyric intensity appropriate to the character and action when accompanied by flute and drums, or serve to emphasize the narration of an accompanying choral chant.[2]

The music also was not of the competitive, ostentatious, decorative kind that Yeats did not, or could not, appreciate:

> Music is the very soul of Nō and shapes the feeling of the audience to the point of imaginative acceptance and participation. Besides the musical accompaniment of drums and flute, which provides a background of rhythmic variety and simple melody, the vocal styles for chanting the lyrical poems which, in turn, constitute the dramatic text, are the basis of the play's composition and structure.[3]

Non-realism, symbolism, restraint of gesture, unobtrusive music, dance, choral lyrics and chanting: Yeats was already committed to all these, and he willingly took over the bare stage, rich costumes and use of masks too.

The Noh also offered a very effective way of presenting the supernatural on stage. Usually the supernatural is hostile, and the protagonist wins his tragic stature by setting up his or her own spiritual values, sometimes unsuccessfully, against this inhuman agent of fate. The dance suggests possession by an unnatural force, and possession, like madness, is always threatening and frightening; likewise, masks are frightening, partly because they eliminate the little facial signals and signs of normal, manageable humanity. Rather than trying to make natural materials look supernatural, there is a suggestion of a hidden dimension *behind* the natural.

In *At the Hawk's Well* (1917) there are only three characters: the Young Man (Cuchulain), the old man, and the Guardian of the Well, a dancer's part, being a girl who never speaks, thus avoiding the perennial problem of finding a professional dancer who could also speak musically. The well, usually dry, occasionally bubbles with water that can give immortality, and although the old man has watched more than fifty years, he has missed each of these upsurgings of magic water because the 'holy shades/That dance upon the desolate mountain' who are 'Deceivers of men' (V 405) have enchanted him into sleep, an enchantment represented in the Guardian's dance. This he tells the young Cuchulain, who has come guided by a rumour, trusting his legendary luck. But the Guardian is possessed by the hawk spirit of the Woman of the Sidhe, whom in her hawk shape Cuchulain has already stoned and antagonised. In the short term the goddess rouses the warrior women of Aoife to religious war against the intruder; in the long term her curse, as the old man suggests, may 'kill your children' or 'You will be so maddened that you kill them with your own hand' (V 408), a fate Yeats had already dramatised in *On Baile's Strand*. Then the action of the play shows the process the old man has described: the Guardian's premonitions of possession presage the arrival of the water of life: she rises and dances, her dance lulling the old man to sleep and luring Cuchulain away off stage, 'as if in a dream' (V 410). Afterwards, his disappointment is realised to the sound of Aoife's warrior women already preparing to attack. 'Stay with me, I have nothing more to lose', appeals the old man, but Cuchulain 'goes out, no longer as if in a dream, but shouldering his spear' (V 412). He may have incurred the Hawk Goddess's curse, but he avoids the trap that has ruined the life of the old man.

So Cuchulain's choice here is different from that of *On Baile's Strand*. His choice of the wandering combative life is not irresponsibility, but a decision to use his life as he wills, not give in to a deceitful goddess's whim. 'I will face them', he cries, choosing positive action. This choice is enigmatically referred to by the chorus of three musicians. Yeats was sometimes ambivalent about the value of the chorus's songs: because one of his objections against music and musical setting was that it obscured the words, he disclaimed interest in the effect: 'Why should not the singer sing something she may wish to have by rote? Nobody will hear the words; and the local timetable . . . would run very nicely with a little management' (E 218). Later he said of the chanting women in *On Baile's Strand*, that though no one would hear the words, 'It seemed right to take some trouble over them, just as it is right to finish off the statue where it is turned to the wall, and besides there is always the reader and one's own pleasure' (V 526). Later still, recalling this, he said 'but singing has changed – I can hear the words – I put my fingers in my ears to keep them out' (V 1008). Here the musicians first call up the scene, otherwise only symbolically evoked by 'a square blue cloth to represent a well' (V 400), then express the conflict of two types, being and becoming:

> The heart would be always awake,
> The heart would turn to its rest.

The heart of the active soul cries 'I would wander always like the wind', while that of the disillusioned man rejoins

Why wander and nothing to find?
Better grow old and sleep. (V 402)

The conflict reaches an ambiguous conclusion in the final chorus, where the musicians prefer 'human faces' to the 'hateful eyes' of the supernatural ones. They choose 'Folly' and are 'content to perish'. But then they praise the man who has settled for a comfortable life, and the heroic Cuchulain, while he has chosen the folly of freedom, has thereby lost 'the comfortable door of his house' and 'children and dogs on the floor'; and while there is comfort in these images there is also ignobility (cows, dogs) though the barrenness of withered tree and dry stones is also undesirable. It seems as though Cuchulain, doomed never to know rest, fixed at last in his heroic destiny, has the best of the bargain after all. This negative endorsement of his choice is, however, difficult for an audience to take in in this concentrated, allusive form, and typically Yeats did not seek to make things easier for the audience by simplifying the presentation.

In *The Only Jealousy of Emer* (1919) likewise, the choruses were not expected to have a direct illumination for the audience: 'sung to modern music in the modern way they suggest strange patterns to the ear without obtruding upon it their difficult irrelevant words' (V 567). The main story is a strong one in its own right, though more complex than *At The Hawk's Well*. It follows immediately after *On Baile's Strand*, so that Cuchulain is lying almost dead after his battle with the waves. His wife Emer and his mistress Eithne Inguba try to call him back to life, but only succeed in calling up the mischief spirit Bricriu. He bargains with Emer for Cuchulain's life, and it is she who has the major tragic choice to make. Bricriu shows her Cuchulain's spirit being tempted in a dance by Fand, the Woman of the Sidhe, his old hawk enemy. As she desires power over Cuchulain, so her rival Bricriu seeks proof of his power over Emer, by requiring her to give up all hopes of regaining Cuchulain's love for ever, as the price of his rescuing him. Emer, a forceful character, resists this demand until she sees Cuchulain's spirit actually follow the Woman of the Sidhe away. She cries out 'I renounce Cuchulain's love for ever', her husband returns to his body, and with bitter irony that shows her sacrifice is real, turns to his mistress Eithne for comfort.

The choruses express one of Yeats's 'philosophic' theories, that the twenty-eight days of the phases of the moon correspond to stages of existence, from more objective to more subjective, the full moon phase at the fifteenth day being the most perfect and least human. Linked with this is the theory of reincarnation, whereby a soul works its way from the most human towards freeing itself into the spirit world, the penultimate stage being that of a person of perfect beauty but minimal humanity. This, apart from being another way of explaining the hard-heartedness of Maud Gonne, shows Eithne as 'a frail, unserviceable thing' in her great beauty, and Fand, over the border in the spirit world, as more destructive still. The beautiful 'statue of solitude', as the chorus rightly says, is a 'bitter reward/Of many a tragic tomb'. These words indicate an unacceptable side to Yeats's theory – that many generations should die virtuously to produce *lack* of virtue. Even if an audience were alert to the theoretical background they might well feel that the simpler message of the first chorus lyric, that 'I will not choose for my friend/A frail unserviceable thing', has an even simpler equivalent in the proverb 'Handsome is as handsome does'; in any case, the main action of the play concentrates on the human struggle of Emer, not the deficiencies of Eithne or Fand.

Although Yeats was proclaimedly writing for a few friends at this time, and 'rejoiced in my freedom from the stupidity of an ordinary audience', his learning after its production of the masks made by the Dutch sculptor van Krop for a performance in Holland inspired him to try to put his play before a large audience. He rewrote it with simplified prose dialogue as *Fighting the Waves* (1929) and incorporated dance and music. This seems a compromise with his avowed dedication to the primacy of words on stage, and there is again a touch of defensiveness in his note:

> I do not say that it is always necessary when one writes for a general audience to make the words of the dialogue so simple and so matter-of-fact; but it is necessary where the appeal is mainly to the eye and to the ear through songs and music. *Fighting the Waves* is in itself nothing, a mere occasion for sculptor and dancer, for the exciting dramatic music of George Antheil. (V 567)

Both these Cuchulain plays show the protagonists asserting human values against the temptations of self-indulgence and the pressures of the non-human world, which could also be seen as fate or circumstance. The masks emphasise the representative nature of their dilemma, but in the other two Plays for Dancers not all the masks seem as appropriate. These plays are *The Dreaming of the Bones* (1919) and *Calvary* (1920). *The Dreaming of the Bones* was written in response to the Easter Rising of 1916, when a small Republican force attempted to declare independence, and occupied and defended the General Post Office in Dublin; several of the leaders were executed by the English after the rising had been put down. In the play the supernatural figures are Diarmuid and Dervorgilla, legendary figures who were supposed to have invited the first invading English force into their country, to support Diarmuid against Dervorgilla's husband who had already defeated him in battle. Their punishment is to wander for ever without being able to kiss, unless some Irish person can be found to forgive them. The human protagonist is unpromising from this point of view, as he is escaping from the Post Office Siege, pursued by the still present English occupying force.

The setting is the bare hills by night in County Clare, but the whole of Ireland is evoked by the fugitive Young Man, with its unroofed houses and devastated towns, its historical development, culture and beauty stunted by the English occupation. Even so, the ghosts' account of their centuries of suffering, expressed also in their dance, wrings the Young Man's heart with pity, yet at the climax of the dance, he reasserts 'never, never/Shall Dairmuid and Dervorgilla be forgiven' (V 775). Yeats has cleverly woven together the legend and its modern relevance in a more direct way than usual: it is typical of Noh drama that the central story should not be enacted but re-enacted, so we do not see the original elopement and betrayal. The universal or particular relevance is left to us, the audience; the past is evoked in narrative and dance; and the Young Man has to apply its relevance to his situation. As in Yeats's *Purgatory*, the introduction of the ghostly dimension of re-enactment and punishment strikes the audience powerfully and poignantly.

The language of this nominally modern play is more

romantic and decorative than the terser speech in *Purgatory*, the Young Man using the advantage of Irish eloquence to move from the immediate impact of

> I was in the Post Office, and if taken
> I shall be put against a wall and shot. (V 764)

to an imaginative defiance of the ghostly world:

> Well, let them dream into what shape they please
> And fill waste mountains with the invisible tumult
> Of the fantastic conscience. (V 766)

His speeches are on the whole more concrete even in their descriptive passages than those of the ghosts, but despite the seven hundred years difference all are speaking in recognisably consistent style. The musicians have their own separate lyrical style, and their song tells of the fascination of becoming absorbed in self-regarding emotions – the 'wandering airy music', linked with night, the curlew and the owl – as opposed to the vigorous active red cocks, the 'strong March birds', with only a hint to indicate that these images are analogous to the ghosts' absorbing but selfish and destructive passion, in conflict with the patriots' active dedication. The analogy is perhaps obscure, but it is more poetically relevant than the moon-reincarnation digressions of *The Only Jealousy of Emer*. The masks also are significantly apportioned, with the ghosts who are fixed in their destiny wearing masks; the Young Man, who is to make a human, unpredestined choice, as well as being a character from the fluctuating present, does not have a mask.

Unfortunately this play, one of Yeats's most integrated and immediate reworkings of Noh form with forceful theme, could not be produced in the difficult political situation following the Rising – even publication was problematic in 1919. Of its later production in 1929, Holloway remarked only that the Young Man was felt to be too commonplace to represent the heroes of the Easter Rising.

Yeats's more esoteric ideas reappeared in *Calvary*, as in the later *Resurrection* where he also develops his own interpretation of the New Testament story. The theme of *Calvary* is simple, however, in that it shows Christ recreating his walk to Calvary and encountering the spirits of Lazarus, Judas and the three Roman soldiers, all of whom reject his redemption. This view of Christ is familiar in Blake: 'Pity would be no more, / If we did not make somebody poor' – Christ needs the need of others to make sense of his divine sacrifice. To Lazarus and Judas, their own autonomy is more important than eternal life. As modern existentialists, they assert the right to choose. The Roman soldiers, less articulately, likewise prefer the freedom of the unredeemed: 'Whatever happens is the best, we say, / So that it's unexpected' (V 786). Their remark 'To know that he has nothing that we need/Must be a comfort to him' is ironic as this very knowledge is a rejection of Christ's purpose, and he cries 'My Father, why has Thou forsaken me?' (V 787). Therefore, masks do not seem appropriate here, as for instance a fixed Judas mask would make nonsense of Judas's ruling motive *not* to be fixed in his role. The Musicians sing first about a self-absorbed, self-hypnotised white heron, and in conclusion about several other birds, following their own individual lives, the refrains of the songs being respectively, 'God has not died for the white heron' and 'God has not appeared to the birds'. In his note, Yeats wrote:

> I have used my bird-symbolism in these songs to increase the objective loneliness of Christ by contrasting it with a loneliness, opposite in kind, that unlike His, can be whether joyous or sorrowful, sufficient to itself. I have surrounded him with the images of those He cannot save, not only with the birds . . . but with Lazarus and Judas and the Roman soldiers for whom He has died in vain . . . I have therefore represented in Lazarus and Judas types of that intellectual despair that lay beyond His sympathy, while in the Roman soldiers I suggest a form of objectivity that lay beyond his help. (V 790).

Suitably, *Calvary* is a kind of reverse Noh play, the last of the sequence in which Yeats had tried out in turn male protagonist, female protagonist, modern protagonist, and disappointed supernatural protagonist. Christ is the son of God, and yet he seems in the position of a human supplicant before the human beings who are now spirits; the dance is danced not by a supernatural tempter, but by the earthy soldiers acting out the role of chance; and the main character does not make a choice because of the re-enactment, but has others' choices cast at him like insults. This play was not produced during Yeats's lifetime, perhaps it was too risky. As for *Resurrection* (1931), which presented the risen Christ as a solid phantom, a contradiction in terms which heralds the end of the cycle of Greek rationality and the beginning of a cycle of mystical irrationality, Yeats feared that its 'subject matter might make it unsuited for the public stage in England or in Ireland' (V 901) but not only was it presented at the Abbey in 1934 but was later produced by E. Martin Browne, Eliot's main producer, with his war-time touring company which specialised in religious plays.

To prove that he could use this form for humour too, Yeats had planned *The Cat and the Moon* (1926) as a kind of 'kyogen' which stood to the Noh something like the Greek satyr play to tragedy. He thought better of this and withheld it from joint publication 'as it was in a different mood' and also commented that it was 'probably unfinished and must remain unfinished until it has been performed and I know how the Lame Man is to move' (V 805). Its dance represents the miraculous curing of the Lame Man's lameness by the saint at a well, where he and the Blind Man who carries him have gone to pray. Like the wise blind man of *On Baile's Strand*, this blind man is materialistic and chooses sight rather than blessedness, and as in the situation in Synge's *The Well of the Saints* discovers how he has been deceived by his companion. The Lame Man is like the earlier Fool in being dishonest but unmaterialistic, and with some misgivings chooses blessedness, after which he is cured of lameness as well, and dances for joy. This charming piece is introduced and closed by the musicians' lyrics about the cat whose complacency is, unknown to him, dominated by the moon.

Yeats's withdrawal into writing plays for the drawing-room and the failure of these to find even a drawing-room production for many years, could have meant the end of his playwriting career. Yet two of his greatest plays were yet to come, *The Words upon the Windowpane*, and *Purgatory*, followed by the less popular but still powerful *The Death of Cuchulain* (1939). Possibly he chose Swift and his life as a more accessible subject for the modern audience, but he gave that subject a Noh form by presenting snatches of Swift's life as re-enacted by a medium at a spiritualist seance. The main emotional conflict is in the tragic relationships of Swift with his women friends Stella and Vanessa, as fragments of transmitted conversation convey, and this serves to convince at least one sceptical attender that the spiritualists' claims are genuine. The final effect, however, is on the audience, for the last sequence takes place after all but the medium have left: as the medium, Mrs Henderson, counts her money and makes her tea, she twice speaks in Swift's voice, once to count his dead friends, once to say 'Perish the day on which I was born!' (V 956). Like the ending of *Calvary*, this conclusion is despairing but gripping. Joseph Holloway reported the play as being a recitation for the medium, and as splendidly played by May Craig. Yeats explained that he himself saw all mediumistic activity however supernatural in appearance as coming mainly from the medium him or her self – as telepathy or telekinesis, that is: supernatural but not coming from a spirit world. This is contrary to the effect of the play where the words of Swift carry great conviction, and later in the same note Yeats added another contradictory view that some manifestations were 'more than transformations of the medium, are, as it were, new beings begotten by spirit upon medium to live short but veritable lives' (V 969).

Yeats was very happy with the popular success of this play, but though it had the aim of reinforcing Irish sense of national identity, culture and tradition by referring to the flowering of Irish civilisation in the eighteenth century, the fact remains that he had not been able to command equal success for the more remote mythic subjects, and moreover this play was in prose, to suit its realistic modern setting.

Purgatory also was to abandon the mythic past for a timeless setting which could be any time in the nineteenth or twentieth century, but first Yeats stubbornly produced two more enigmatic dance plays and a third blackly comic Noh-style play based on Irish legend. Both the dance plays centre on a Salome-like dance before a severed head, with symbolic and perverted overtones of sexuality. First written in prose, *The King of the Great Clock Tower* (1935) shows a Pinteresque encounter between a weak king, his silent queen and a presumptuous stroller, the latter being beheaded but somehow seeming to win by evoking more reaction from the mysterious queen than the king can; it was rewritten in verse, then the new version, *A Full Moon in March* (1935), eliminates the king and presents a confrontation between swineherd and queen, now a speaking part. The baffling and destructive nature of sexual conflict underlies all versions and this, like the supernatural possession of earlier plays, seems to impel the characters against their human personality; the symbolism includes some of Yeats's favourite images, such as the Grecian-urn-like picture of ever-running deer and maiden with apple, or the king's clock, representing eternity and time. The musicians' lyrics are even more 'difficult' than usual, but the images of the closing song of *The King of the Great Clock Tower*, which include a 'rambling, shambling man' and 'wicked, crooked, hawthorn tree', and lovely ladies dancing in a ruined castle though all are 'blown cold dust or a bit of bone' take us directly on to *Purgatory*.

The main character of *Purgatory* (1939) is an old 'travelling man' who with his son returns to the ruin of the great house where he was born; at the climax of the play the ruins light up and we see, not dancing, but the re-enactment of the Old Man's degraded groom father coming to his mother's room on their wedding night. The passion that led to her misalliance was a sin which led to more sin and ruin, for she died in giving birth to the Old

Man, who grew up to avenge the ill treatment of his brutal father by stabbing him to death in the burning house. At first the son cannot see the ghosts; his father tries to explain the vicious circle of this re-enactment of the fatal moment of passion – its repetition is a punishment for the pleasure, a pleasure which is renewed with each repetition, and so has again to be punished by repetition, and so on. The son ignores this – he is more interested in stealing the Old Man's bag of money, and their struggle over the bag raises the tension between them. At this point the son sees the lighted window and ghosts in the ruin, involving him in the chain of consequences, and as he reels in fear his father stabs him, with the same knife which killed his own father. The Old Man has reasoned that with this death he has 'finished all that consequence' and released his mother's soul into peace. But the recommencement of the re-enactment as he turns to go proves that he has failed. He is 'Twice a murderer and all for nothing': at last, his only recourse is the mercy of God, to whom he addresses the final lines

> Mankind can do no more. Appease
> The misery of the living and the remorse of the dead.
> (V 1049)

There are no songs in this play, and no masks, but the central interaction of past and present forms the action, and the set, with its ruined doorway and the bare trees – possibly a 'wicked, crooked, hawthorn tree' – meets the Noh criteria of simplicity and minimal representation. Here Yeats's four-stress verse, admired by Eliot, accommodates the Old Man's occasional imagery: the tree he remembers has 'Green leaves, ripe leaves, leaves thick as butter, / Fat greasy life' (V 1042) representing the repellent physical passion of his parents' youth, and now in the moonlight 'All cold, sweet, glistening light', like the spiritual purity he wrongly hopes he has gained for his mother's soul. The verse also gives to his narrative a driving force that suits the inexorable unfolding of these entwined, predestined stories, and *Purgatory* played to enthusiastic appreciation from the audience, who found the strong situation and the dramatic shock of the unexpected murder absorbing.

Yeats had said that the modern taste was for comedy, but his supernatural tragedy was more to the taste of the Abbey directors than his comedy *The Herne's Egg* (1938), which they rejected. Yeats claimed to be relieved by this decision: 'I am no longer fit for riots and I thought a bad riot almost certain' (L 871). Though the hero Congal dies at the end and there is a multiple rape of the heroine, the play is neither appalling nor offensive, as these features might suggest. Congal tries to assert human commonsense against the bird god, the great Herne, and is even less successful than Cuchulain had been at the Hawk's Well. Congal's initial offence is to take sacred heron's eggs for his feast, and when through the priestess Attracta's agency the feast is turned into insult and fighting, Congal's decision that Attracta must lose her evident madness, due to sexual frustration, by lying with seven men, recognised in the play as a well-known cure, is motivated partly by revenge on the god through the priestess his bride, and partly by folk superstition. Attracta is in a trance, and in the next scene claims that not the men but the Herne himself lay with her, a statement confirmed by supernatural thunder. Congal tries his best to resist this supernatural lie, and to escape the Herne's curse that he shall be killed by a fool, but all is in vain, and as a final insult he is reincarnated in the body of a donkey. Congal is an attractive character – more, as he says, the old campaigner than the legendary king – and there are several engaging stage effects, such as the ritualistic battle presented in silhouette, the giant toy donkey led by Attracta's servant, the chorus of Congal's chief soldiers, with their homely names, who do not actually wish to rape the priestess, offering excuses such as 'I am promised to an educated girl. Her family are most particular . . .' (V 1028). The verse is the four-stress, crisp, urgent form, carrying the plot along at a business-like pace, which more than in *The Green Helmet* suggests an undercurrent of danger and terror beneath the practical actions of the characters.

The Death of Cuchulain (1939), however, returns to blank verse for its medium. Written at the same time as the poem 'Cuchulain Comforted' the play was the last piece of work on which Yeats was working at the time of his death. As if Cuchulain were finally drowning in the waves, figures from his past life appear before him, first his mistress Eithne Inguba with a message to him to go out and fight impossible odds – supposed to be from his wife Emer, but in fact a lying enchantment from his enemies – then Aoife, now an old woman, recalling their battle and love at the Hawk's Well, and his later killing of their son on Baile's Strand, then the Blind Man who blindly witnessed that combat. Like any aging man, Cuchulain is bound by his years and deeds to mortality, as Aoife binds him to a pillar, while he admits that she has the right to kill him, and he is content to die. The Blind Man kills him, the Morrigu (the War Goddess) chronicles his last battle and his wounds at the hands of six warriors, and Emer's final dance expresses the rage at waste and glory of achievement to mark the death of a great hero. The crux of the play, however, is that it is the degraded, money-seeking Blind Man who kills Cuchulain, *not* Aoife. It is the final levelling, sordid aspect of death, not camouflaged by poetic justice, that Yeats wished to stress. This conclusion comments with Euripidean bitterness on the way fate and mankind treat heroes. The irony is reinforced by the framing of the myth with a prologue from an irascible old man who laments 'this vile age', and an epilogue from three street singers with 'music of some Irish Fair of our day'. The singer compares the heroes of the past, perfect but now an insubstantial memory, with the solid men of today who lack heroism, and asks whether these solid men are the 'sole reality'. She refers to the Post Office Siege, and suggests the spirit of Cuchulain was there effectively if not tangibly. The lines:

> But an old man looking on life
> Imagines it in scorn (V 1063)

seem to sum up Yeats's motives in picturing his heroic characters – to sting into life the unheroic modern Irishman. Cuchulain is weary and willing to die, but his mode of death is an indictment of materialistic man.

Though there is a strong sense that Cuchulain's death is given significance by his past deeds – the prologue tells the audience 'they must know the old epics and Mr. Yeats's plays' (V 1051) – the past is not recreated during the play, and the action is in the present. This has been Yeats's tendency in all the Noh plays, and even in the pre-Noh plays such as *Deirdre* and *On Baile's Strand* where a past crisis has produced a belated consequence. Richard Taylor noted that 'in the western sense of the world, the ritual of Nō is not really dramatic' and though such plays as *Waiting for Godot* have notoriously expanded our definition of the dramatic, Yeats's adding an element of present action to the re-enactment both increases its acceptability by western audiences, and mirrors the relationship of play and audience's everyday life: as the protagonists absorb and make the appropriate reaction to the past situation – whether it is a magic well, a husband's enchantment, betrayal to the invaders – so the audience is to absorb and react to the play.

4
Eliot: 'Murder in the Cathedral' and its Predecessors

> I believe that the theatre has reached a point at which a revolution in principles should take place. (SE 109)

After his years of study at Harvard, Eliot proceeded on a one-year fellowship to Europe, planning to work on his thesis on the philosopher F. H. Bradley at Oxford. Less than a year later he married Vivienne Haigh-Wood, an upper-middle-class girl of volatile temperament, not to say unstable personality, whose instability may have had its origin in her imperfectly understood ill-health.

Doctors and treatment for Vivienne, plus the expense of a married household, pushed Eliot into gainful, secure, regular employment with all its constraints. He settled to giving normal working hours to his job as clerk at Lloyds Bank, two stints at schoolteaching having proved his irremovable dislike for such work; he then spent his evenings writing poetry and criticism. 'Prufrock' had been circulated to friends and acquaintances privately, but with its publication in 1917 Eliot's name became established in literary circles, where he became a considerable figure quite quickly, accumulating reviewing, lecturing and editing work, and being asked to write for the *Times Literary Supplement* by 1919. All this was necessarily more of a strain for him than for his Bloomsbury contemporaries, most of whom pursued their literary efforts supported by parents or private incomes, and only during three months' paid leave, granted on medical grounds to avert a threatening breakdown, could he find time to write 'The Waste Land'. In the same year that this was published, 1922, Eliot also began to edit, in his 'spare time', *The Criterion*, financed by Lady Rothermere. Fortunately the pressure of this situation was relieved when a friend interested the publisher Geoffrey Faber in Eliot: Faber took over the support of *The Criterion* when Lady Rothermere withdrew from it, and also offered Eliot a more remunerative, more secure and less exhausting job as editor with his firm.

So far, Eliot had not apparently experimented practically in writing plays, but he seems to have been working on the fragments and drafts of *Sweeney Agonistes* during the 1920s. The published fragments of *Sweeney* were once regarded as poetic but undramatic, or at best a dead end, but now many critics see not only 'contemporary relevance' and 'colloquial speech', two of Eliot's proclaimed goals, but also dramatic effectiveness in these passages. Curiously Arnold Bennett, whose solid naturalistic novels could hardly be more foreign to Eliot's associative, elliptical work, was a confidant at the genesis of *Sweeney*:

> I said I couldn't see the point of the poem (The Waste Land). He said he didn't mind what I said as he had definitely given up that form of writing, and was now

centred on dramatic writing. He wanted to write a drama of modern life (furnished flat sort of people) in a rhythmic prose 'perhaps with certain things in it accentuated by drum-beats'. And he wanted my advice. We arranged that he should do the scenario and some sample pages of dialogue.[1]

The 'furnished flat' people are Doris and Dusty, and in this flat, paid for by Pereira, an offstage, sinister telephone voice, we see other people including Sweeney himself. These characters or similar ones also appear in Eliot's poetry as shallow, rootless figures whose modernity is a substitute for firm beliefs and values. The nearest the girls come to religious beliefs is in casting their fortune with playing cards, and Sweeney's attempt to express the mystery of life and death and the feelings of someone responsible for bringing death by violence – introduced by 'I knew a man once done a girl in' – is anchored firmly in the sordid and the contemporary

> Well he kept her there in a bath
> With a gallon of lysol in a bath (CPP 124)

The prose with drum beats became rhythmic verse that was more colloquial than anything in the later plays and, far from disguising itself as everyday speech, the language aggressively draws attention to its rhythmic qualities:

> SWEENEY: Nobody came
> And nobody went
> But he took in the milk and he paid the rent
> SWARTS: What did he do?
> All that time, what did he do?

SWEENEY: What did he do! what did he do?
That don't apply.
Talk to live men about what they do.
He used to come and see me sometimes
I'd give him a drink and cheer him up.
DORIS: Cheer him up?
DUSTY: Cheer him up?
SWEENEY: Well here again that don't apply
But I've gotta use words when I talk to you.
(CPP 124–5)

The repetition characteristic of Eliot's poetic style is here like the verbal menace of later Pinter, and the empty gestures imitating communication similarly prefigure the ineffectual conversations of Pinter's characters or Beckett's:

DUSTY: It's a funny thing how I draw court cards –
DORIS: There's a lot in the way you pick them up
DUSTY: There's an awful lot in the way you feel
DORIS: Sometimes they'll tell you nothing at all
DUSTY: You've got to know what you want to ask them
DORIS: You've got to know what you want to know
DUSTY: It's no use asking them too much
DORIS: It's no use asking more than once
DUSTY: Sometimes they're no use at all. (CPP 118)

The unfinished state of the fragments means that the menace in the dialogue remains unfocused; the characters are menaced by Pereira's telephone call, by the fortune-telling cards and by Sweeney's story of the murder – it is not clear, though some have assumed it, whether Sweeney is the murderer himself. Hugh Kenner suggests that the fragments are self-contained as they stand, but other draft fragments existed. In a letter Eliot included more material, and the programme of a 1965 staged tribute to Eliot included not only this additional material but dialogue bringing on stage Mrs Porter, a lady mentioned in connection with Sweeney in 'The Waste Land'. Here the dialogue got more than drumbeats, as Katharine Worth describes:

> There is a sustained threat in the verse rhythms, balanced as they are, and as the Dankworth production well brought out, on the edge of a great jazz explosion which powerfully suggests the emotional explosion to which the action must move.[2]

The jazz, like the poetry, was justified here, for Eliot's subtitle 'Fragments of an Aristophanic Melodrama' not only bows to the common use of melodrama as a crude and often horrific drama but also to its original sense of drama with music; the American characters acting as chorus sing slightly parodied and again rather menacing popular songs. This framework of black comedy presented defiant exuberant satire without the protective colouring of realistic style; Eliot seems to have been in touch with the spirit of his age more firmly here than later, but for some reason at this period his work broke down, and he felt that inspiration for all poetry, lyric as well as dramatic, had dried up permanently. When he began to write again, inspiration had evidently revived, but not for works which one could call exuberant.

Possibly the drama of his own life preoccupied him: his decision to separate from his wife Vivienne in 1933 preceded his next burst of dramatic writing, though other personal developments also had an influence. At this time Eliot had recently been received into the Church of

England (in 1927), after the youthful years of agnosticism that had succeeded the Unitarianism of his upbringing. Among the friends he made were those interested in religious drama.

The movement had been growing since the turn of the century, and a major impulse towards a new religious drama probably came from rediscovering the old religious drama of the mystery, miracle and morality plays. The important director William Poel's production of *Everyman* in 1901 was seminal here, and other productions followed: one of Poel's actors, Nugent Monck, founded the Norwich Players in 1910, who at their Maddermarket Theatre specialised in mediaeval religious drama. Amateurs were inspired to write simpler new plays for their local churches, and before the First World War a Morality Play Society flourished. More significant were the festivals which began to appear on a larger scale. Some, like the Glastonbury festival, its productions ranging from the choral drama *Bethlehem* by Richard Boughton in 1915 to A. E. Housman's St Francis plays in 1922, were regular events, whereas others, such as the celebration of Exeter Cathedral's octocentenary, were single occasions. Where most of the minor and provincial amateur works were of little interest dramatically, the larger festivals attracted established and talented writers and made them attempt a new genre or style.

The Canterbury festival was one of the most important of these, and the most important figure in the movement was George Bell, who as Dean of Canterbury first asked John Masefield to write his *The Coming of Christ* in 1928. The success of this led to the inauguration of the Canterbury festival in 1929; at first established plays were put on, such as Tennyson's *Becket* in 1932, then profits were used to commission new plays, of which *Murder in the Cathedral* was the first in 1935. Simultaneously with the first festival, the Religious Drama Society was formed and George Bell became president, though he now had to leave Canterbury to become Bishop of Chichester. In 1930 he appointed E. Martin Browne as his Director of Religious Drama, in charge of a semi-professional company called the Chichester Dioscesan Players. At this point, T. S. Eliot came in contact with the religious drama movement.

E. Martin Browne is another key figure in the development both of religious and of poetic drama at this period. Well known as Eliot's director, he also promoted and directed the work of new and established poetic dramatists, including Yeats. During the war he toured with his own small company, the Pilgrim players, specialising in religious drama, and later put on a season of poetic drama at the Mercury theatre to encourage new verse dramatists. His detailed account of the genesis, growth and productions of Eliot's plays is invaluable, and he played a large part in encouraging Eliot to make the move into dramatic writing in the first place.

Browne describes his first meeting with Eliot at a weekend houseparty organised by the Bishop of Chichester in the hopes of engaging Eliot in religious drama – hopes which must have foundered in the unforthcoming, if not downright forbidding attitude of his guest. Eliot 'did not join much in the conversation', and after he had read aloud his poem 'Ash Wednesday' to the company, Browne remembered, 'there was a long silence; our hesitating attempts to talk about the poem were not at all assisted by the author, who always believed that a work of art must speak for itself' (EMB 2). However, Browne's own experience in producing such things as pageants led to his being consulted about a fund-raising dramatic project in London (the funds were to build no fewer than forty-five churches in the expanding Greater London suburbs) and then to his persuading the committee to accept Eliot as the ideal writer to transform the conventional pageant idea into something outstanding. Against the objections that Eliot was 'too modern, too difficult' Browne was confident of his choice:

> He was, first of all, the major poet of his time, and in a sense in which that description can rarely be applied. He had re-formed the language of poetry, and every creative mind among English writers was under his influence, every young person awakening to the value of words found a special value in *his* words. His was the distinctive voice of the age.
>
> And it was at the same time the voice of a prophet. . . . For it was the voice of one who had very lately, after a long and agonising struggle, found rest in the faith of the English Church. This faith, therefore, meant passionately more to him than to most of those who had always had it. He was also a highly skilled craftsman, willing, in order to learn at first hand a new part of his craft, to submit to the regimen imposed by a commission, and to work for a specific and limited purpose. (EMB 6)

This analysis indicates what, at that time, Eliot's support for poetic drama as well as for religious drama would mean to the audience. For Eliot, then, this was a learning process. His tone when he was given the job of writing *The Rock*, as the episodic work came to be titled, was neither exuberant nor enthusiastic: 'The task was clearly laid out: I had only to write the words of prose dialogue for scenes of the usual historical pageant pattern, for which I had been given a scenario' (3VP 7), adding that he hoped that the need to meet a deadline would operate where mere inspiration had failed. The subject matter was to be church building and destruction over the centuries, and Browne had begun a scenario that pulled several episodes together as flashbacks within the framework of a modern church-building project. Eliot was one of a team involved in the production, but he was one of the least experienced in the theatre, and learnt largely by watching other people's efforts, attending only the later rehearsals.

> He was a very silent witness. This was not only due to his strong sense of theatre-decorum. He was never one to offer comment on things with which he was not fully acquainted; he confined himself to the plea of every author: 'I wish they would speak my lines exactly as I wrote them', and to points on the reading of the verse. It was not till several years and several plays later than he would discuss points of production with me during rehearsal. (EMB 11)

So, though Eliot did have some contact with the theatrical process from this early stage, evidently his rather semi-detached relationship to the huge, disparate, unwieldy, amateur, *ad hoc* company did not, any more than his advisory relationship to later professional casts, give him the sort of long-continuing, developing association that luckier playwrights were able to set up with permanent companies. This is obviously important to a writer who is trying to develop new style and subject matter, to be able to afford to make mistakes and try again. A writer such as Shaw, on the other hand, who is as it were putting new wine in old bottles and insinuating his message under the guise of established comic forms, can rely on his company's training in these forms. As Eliot began to write with a prospect not only of the 'unknown audience' but of 'unknown actors rehearsed by an unknown producer' (SP 76) he had to consider what his company was likely to do without his really being able to influence them very much.

One of the problems is described with restraint by Browne:

> I was offered the services of Vincent Howson, the vicar of an East End parish who had formerly been a member of Sir Frank Benson's famous Shakespearian Company. . . . He was very keen both to offer his own professional skill and to bring in a group of his amateurs to play these scenes with him. But he was faced with 'a grave difficulty' as he pointed out to me in a long letter dated 29 March 1934 (only two months before the opening). He felt that Mr. Eliot's dialogue was 'not true cockney . . .' (EMB 14)

and in the end 'we had to allow Mr. Howson to adjust his part – and with it, to some extent, the others – to suit himself'. Hence Eliot's disclaimer in a note that Mr Howson had so rewritten the dialogue that he should be considered joint author. The sample of unadjusted dialogue given by Browne is less objectionable for any isolated non-cockney turns of phrase than in the improbable cogency, elaboration, organisation and fluency of the workman Ethelbert ('Bert') in exhorting his mates, in spite of its top dressing of 'if you take my meanings' and 'in a manner of speakings'. Unlike Sweeney, Bert has no problem in using words in instant oratory; but his mate Albert, a more modern furnished flat sort of person potentially if not financially, has lines which are not only more convincing but have clear echoes of Sweeney's repetition, with the verse rhythm carefully blurred:

> ALFRED: Well, I can't see as it makes any difference to you or me whether it's a church or a bank. You don't get paid any more for building a church nor a bank, do you? I get my money just the same, and that's all the same to me. (EMB 15)

The actual scene of which Eliot acknowledged authorship was that in which rival groups of fascists and communists seek to proselytise and demoralise the church-building christians. The Blackshirts have a bouncing rhyming verse:

> Our methods are new in this land of the free
> We make the deaf hear and we make the blind see.
> We're law-keeping fellows who make our own laws –
> And we welcome SUBSCRIPTIONS IN AID OF THE CAUSE!
> (R 44)

while the Redshirts self-consciously parody a 'precious' kind of free verse:

> Our verse
> is free
> as the wind on the steppes
> as love in the heart of the factory worker
> thousands and thousands of steppes
> millions and millions of workers
> all working
> all loving (R 43)

Eliot himself thought he learnt most from writing for the Chorus, if in a negative way: 'Its members were speaking *for me*, not uttering words that really represented any supposed character of their own' (3VP 7). And while there is a hint of the style of Eliot's later poetry, especially in vocabulary and repetition, the tone is uncertain, and the contrast of traditional rhetoric and incongruous vulgar imagery does not satirise 'the modern' as confidently as his earlier poems:

> A thousand policemen directing the traffic
> Cannot tell you why you come or where you go.
> A colony of cavies or a horde of active marmots
> Build better than they that build without the LORD.
> Shall we lift up our feet among perpetual ruins?
> I have loved the beauty of Thy House, the peace of thy
> Sanctuary,
> I have swept the floors and garnished the
> altars. (CPP 155)

The changing point of view is more confusing in a spoken chorus than in lyric verse, and the 'you', 'they', 'we' and 'I' add to the problem of the Chorus speaking for itself or for Eliot. Condemnation is weakened from such a wavering speaker, and this Eliot recognised in making his next chorus specifically the 'Women of Canterbury'.

The Rock, put on in London at the Sadler's Wells theatre, received a lot of press attention, so Eliot's interest in religious drama was widely known. The commission for *Murder in the Cathedral* followed from his first attempt, and this time he had full control over his plot and material.

His account of the action of *Murder in the Cathedral* (1935) is deprecatory: 'A man comes home, foreseeing that he will be killed, and he is killed', and action that he considers 'somewhat limited', although one could say as much about, say, Aeschylus's *Agamemnon*. Eliot in fact while hammering out his new poetic drama, characteristically kept a grasp on Western dramatic tradition. As in Greek tragedy, there is a sense of inevitability in the progress of his hero towards his doom, but here the inevitability points to a 'pattern' which has a specific Christian religious message: the inevitable pattern is that of God's will for mankind, and the Christian subject's free will comes into play as he chooses whether to accept or ignore that pattern. Christ is the exemplar of submission to God's will, and in this play Thomas à Becket's martyrdom shows his achievement of the imitation of Christ in enacting the pattern of God's will.

The tension implicit in this gradual progress towards tragic climax is strong throughout the play. Thomas, Archbishop of Canterbury, arrives at his cathedral from France determined to resist the submission of church to state that King Henry demands. The result must be his destruction, and he undergoes a series of temptations, testing his determination. The chorus of the Women of Canterbury express the related anguish of the whole community, frightened by the chaotic forces that seem to be tearing at their world, deprived of reason or divine purpose. Becket's victory over the tempters is only a temporary release of tension, and the physical threat of the four Knights, come to assassinate Becket the turbulent priest, implicates the audience in the brutality and political expediency of the murder. The chorus's concluding thanksgiving for Thomas's testimony through martyrdom sends the audience away in a subdued if thoughtful mood. The Catharsis of pity and terror has been harnessed to recognition of God's terrible but productive pattern.

The first production in Canterbury cathedral chapter house impressed audiences far beyond the cultural endurance that Eliot modestly suggested as their motive. The chapter house stage, specially built, was shallow and had no exits, so that actors came and went through the audience or had to stay put on stage. Against the rhythmic shapes of the arcading with its painted decoration in 'cold colours' the actors stood out through their vivid costumes – the monks in Benedictine robes of black, the tempters in yellow, the chorus in green with red and blue patterns. This brilliance, designed both to conform and compete with the cathedral's decoration of stained glass, hangings and painted arcading, in Martin Browne's view 'restricted the Chorus to their liturgical function in the play, and prevented the development of that other aspect, "the poor, the poor women of Canterbury"' (EMB 63). The effect was more like the colourist experiments of Yeats than, say, the neutral sombre hues used by the 1972 Aldwych production. Becket was played by Robert Speaight, actor, novelist, biographer and critic, who was an experienced verse speaker, won universal praise, and became identified with the play, and with religious drama roles generally.

Eliot made the limitation of his plot into the keystone of a very tight unity of theme and expression in the play, building its simple strong structure upon the 'returns . . . is killed' outline. There are no subplots and no extraneous characters or counterpointed themes. The opening of the play follows the austerity of Greek tragedy rather than the multi-level development of Shakespearean tragedy and history, though there are reminiscences of both. The chorus of the Women of Canterbury strikes a note of anticipation:

> Some presage of an act
> Which our eyes are compelled to witness, has forced
> our feet
> Towards the cathedral. We are forced to bear
> witness. (CPP 239)

The first exposition scene is of a form often used by Shakespeare, with three minor characters, priests of Canterbury, expanding on the hints given by the chorus and interrupted by a messenger introducing a new element, the return of the exiled archbishop Thomas Becket. However, the development of this main conflict, in that Thomas is openly defying King Henry by returning, is not filled in dramatically and explored in the accumulative chronicle scenes that Shakespeare might have used. Though Thomas's besetting sin is pride, Eliot is not primarily concerned with psychological analysis. The crux of the play is that Thomas should truly submit to the will of God, regardless of his particular flaws of character. Thus, unlike other writers on this historical event, Eliot has not dramatised the process whereby Thomas comes to face martyrdom; not his life, but his attitude to death is Eliot's concern here, and Thomas's pride, while it rounds his personality, is of importance only in the first part and as a factor which may impair his own will to do right. Pride is a flaw, but not a fatal flaw.

The conflicts, then, are less of character than of values. The form Eliot adopts here is like that of Milton's *Samson Agonistes*, which he admired, and even more similar to Yeats's *On the King's Threshold*: a series of tempters oppose other values to Becket's dedication to what he sees as God's will. Their danger lies in their proved attraction to Becket – all have appealed to him at some time or other, and so the tempters also have a second function of presenting indirectly, and as it were by reflection, former phases of Thomas's personality.

Eliot tries to bring his tempters forward in ascending order of persuasiveness: the first one, in the guise of a friend of youth, is a comparatively mild test, offering a return to the simple worldly pleasures of those days, no longer very attractive to Thomas, though he remarks 'The impossible is still temptation' (CPP 248). This tempter's farewell 'Your Lordship is too proud . . ./I leave you to the pleasures of your higher vices,/Which will have to be paid for at higher prices' (CPP 248) hints at his continuing weakness. The second and third tempters are perhaps too equal in weight: the second tempter urges not only the undeniable good Thomas could do if reconciled with King Henry and reinstated in his former chancellorship, but also the relationship between the now estranged friends. The form of Thomas's rejection of worldly power, scorning it by comparison with his ecclesiastical power 'supreme alone in England' (CPP 250) again indicates the ominous tendency to spiritual pride. After this, the third tempter, a baron who was once Thomas's enemy, moves the forces of the power struggle into a different relationship. He suggests an alliance between barons and archbishop to secure the religious power of Thomas's position against the king, an alliance 'At once, for England and for Rome' (CPP 252). This alliance with a former enemy seems less inviting than the previous temptation, but it does uncover an uglier motive, as Thomas recognises and rejects:

> To make, then break, this thought has come before,
> The desperate exercise of failing power.
> Samson in Gaza did no more. (CPP 252)

In the Bible as in folk tales, temptations come in threes; thus both Thomas and the audience are surprised when Eliot produces a fourth tempter. This sinister personage confirms Thomas's rejection of the previous tempters and advises him to 'Fare forward to the end' on 'the way already chosen' (CPP 253), advice Thomas understandably finds disconcerting. The fourth tempter is the spokesman of Thomas's hidden self, 'tempting me with my own desires' (CPP 253), and addresses him intimately as 'Thomas' where the others had said 'My lord'. He presents even the upholding of the will of God as motivated by a sinful grasping after self-glorification by martyrdom.

> Is there no way, in my soul's sickness,
> Does not lead to damnation in pride? (CPP 255)

cries Thomas. The crisis drives him to a deeper examination of his own will. He is silent while the tempters, priests and Women of Canterbury comment on the predicament of himself and mankind in general. Then he returns for a long last speech summarising his life and its temptations.

> Thirty years ago, I searched all the ways
> That lead to pleasure, advancement and praise . . .
> Ambition comes when early force is spent
> And when we find no longer all things possible . . .
> Servant of God has chance of greater sin
> And sorrow, than the man who serves a king
> For those who serve the greater cause may make the
>   cause serve them,
> Still doing right. (CPP 258)

Recognising this danger, he has painfully worked out his salvation:

> The last temptation is the greatest treason:
> To do the right thing for the wrong reason.
> (CPP 258)

The only solution is by self-abnegation: to do the right thing for the right reason, and trust in God's power.

The first part ends with Thomas's achievement of this assurance, and before the second part, there is an 'Interlude' in the form of a prose sermon, in which he emphasises his own renunciation of will:

> A martyrdom is always the design of God, for His love of men, to warn them and to lead them, to bring them back to His ways. It is never the design of man; for the true martyr is he who has become the instrument of God, who has lost his will in the will of God, and who no longer desires anything for himself, not even the glory of being a martyr. (CPP 261)

There is no wavering after this, and the second part of the play shows symmetrically the arrival of the four Knights, their menaces, attack and murder of the archbishop, followed by their prose defence of the deed. The audience might well feel that the real conflict was over once Thomas has come to terms with his own motives, and that the second part can only be a crude enactment of the inevitable end. However, Becket's culminating speech in part one, where he steps outside his own drama, 'What yet remains to show you of my history' (CPP 258), to address the audience, points to the new thematic emphasis of the rest of the action. He has shown the struggles, errors and final acceptance that every man could or should pass through if such a trial were imposed on him; now, as the emphasis moves to the wider significance of Thomas's martyrdom, the chorus and priests learn the meaning that another's sacrifice can have for them. For every evil, Becket tells the audience,

> . . . you, and you,
> And you, must all be punished. So must you.
> (CPP 259)

The Women of Canterbury in their role as chorus continually express by their exclamations of horror the fact that this is not just a political assassination, but an epitome of all the evil that man is capable of – always, man falls away from his spiritual nature, but, unable to share the amoral indifference of the animals, remains fully aware of his degradation:

> United to the spiritual flesh of nature
> Mastered by the animal powers of spirit,
> Dominated by the lust of self-demolition,
> By the final utter uttermost death of spirit,
> By the final ecstasy of waste and shame. (CPP 271)

As representatives of humanity, they contain within themselves at the same time guilt for the human capacity for evil, and revulsion at this degradation. Their anguish at their 'share of the eternal burden' prompts a speech of comfort from the archbishop; not only will their pain be compensated by 'a sudden painful joy' when 'God's purpose is made complete' but, as this level of awareness cannot be sustained for long, both pain and joy will lose their immediacy in memory: 'Human kind cannot bear very much reality' (CPP 271). Nonetheless, they have to participate in the spiritual experience, and this is why repeated martyrdoms are necessary, so that human beings never sink too far into the animal torpor of 'Living and partly living'.

Here the liturgical aspect of the play is evident. The mass celebrated by Becket during the play is reflected by the play, in that both remember Christ's sacrifice and the audience's implication in it. In his earlier 'Dialogue on Poetic Drama' (1928) one of the dialogue's disputants, 'E', who may stand for Eliot himself, suggests that to revive poetic drama the solution is 'to return to religious liturgy'. To this another participant, 'B' returns a flat 'No': pointing out the difference between the real-life involvement of the communicant and the imaginative involvement of the audience, he says 'religion is no more a substitute for drama than drama is a substitute for religion' (SE 48). In *Murder in the Cathedral* Eliot is approaching liturgy in two ways – by including it as a natural part of the action, and by basing the play's own equivalent structure upon it.

Another level of significance underlies the choral speeches here: the sense of impurity, dislocation, doom is presented as a primitive fear of the inexplicable. Where the festival chorus had, as Browne said, fulfilled a liturgical function enacting sin and guilt, the 1972 Aldwych production brought out this more primitive emotion by the wilder expression of the speakers, insisting on their reactions. By the 1970s, theatregoers were familiar with various plays of savage ritual, and the production sought to yoke the primitive theme with the equally strong Christian emphases.

The chorus always has a vital function in representing both guilt and rejection of evil on behalf of the audience and of mankind generally, and in spite of his later misgivings about its dramatic success, it had been fundamental to Eliot's conception of the play. He began from the position that he wanted to show what modern secular man tended to ignore, 'the primacy of the supernatural over the natural life' (SP 42), and to force this home by insisting on its 'contemporary relevance' (SP 77). The chorus therefore relates the crucial importance of a sense of divine purpose to the natural life of the community, which through the ritual of the church is implied to be of continuing importance over the centuries, while the Knights press home the 'contemporary relevance' by more explicit means.

The Knights have a more specific, less universal role in this particular martyrdom, and by their direct address to the audience they insist by more logical argument on the audience's share in their guilt. The Knights appeal, across the centuries, to 'hard-headed sensible people', who therefore realise where hard-headedness may lead them. Gradually they implicate the audience by striking the familiar note of a thousand public meetings: 'I think we will all agree . . . You will agree with me that . . . Morville has given us a great deal to think about . . . Need I say more?' (CPP 276–9). At another level from that of the emotional women, the Knights relate the murder to common experience, where materialistic, this-worldly, commonsensical reasons weigh more heavily in the balance than spiritual values. In ordinary life, the unfortunate results of pragmatic decisions can be ignored, but here we have just seen the brutal on-stage murder and the responsibility of those who accept pragmatic values is stressed: 'if there is any guilt whatever in the matter, you must share it with us' (CPP 279).

Structurally, the coda-like speeches of priests and

chorus that follow the Knights' apologia bring about the reconciliation of the conflicts of the play. The will of God is accepted by priests and chorus, and the martyrdom, briefly lamented, as is natural – 'The Church lies bereft' – is then also accepted; the Church is not defeated, but 'supreme, so long as men will die for it' (CPP 280). The chorus in a kind of Benedicite affirm the coherent, God-ordained pattern:

> For all things exist only as seen by Thee, only as
> known by Thee, all things exist
> Only in Thy light, and Thy glory is declared even in
> that which denies Thee; the darkness declares the
> glory of light. (CPP 281)

Thanking God for the death of Thomas, therefore, the Women conclude by acknowledging their part in the martyrdom,

> That the sin of the world is upon our heads; that the
> blood of the martyrs and the agony of the saints
> Is upon our heads. (CPP 283)

Eliot then has succeeded in writing a play which deals with 'the primacy of the supernatural over the natural life', and by its structure, which 'opens out' the theme of the first part into the second part, has given it 'contemporary relevance' as well as universal relevance. His ambition to prove the worth of poetry on stage is convincingly supported by his writings for the chorus: other dramatists have used more economic and allusive ways of evoking horror and disorientation, but here the elaborate, glutted, intense description of experience that

Eliot wanted is presented by language we must call poetic. Indeed, the feeling and atmosphere are the more successfully realised because Eliot is not handicapped by the need to imitate 'ordinary speech': the long lines pile image upon image in excess of disgust:

> I have seen
> Grey necks twisting rats tails twining, in the thick
> light of dawn. I have eaten
> Smooth creatures still living, with the strong salt taste
> of living things under the sea; I have tasted
> The living lobster, the crab, the oyster, the whelk and
> the prawn; and they live and spawn in my bowels, and
> my bowels dissolve in the light of dawn. (CPP 270)

As Stevie Smith remarked, 'One observes how the poetry mounts at each touch of pain and sinks when, as does not often happen, something agreeable comes to mind'.[3] This grotesquerie, particularly in the move from the general smooth creatures to the specific whelks and prawns, borders on the ludicrous and needs the insistent tone of the poetic context to press home Eliot's vision of horror when the ludicrous becomes hideous, whereas in *The Family Reunion* the modern conversational tone of the verse undermines a similar attempt to use 'The noxious smell untraceable in the drains' as an image of fear. Both verse form and the level of emotion are varied, so that the lamentation and repetition of

> O late late late, late is the time, late too late, and
> rotten the year
> Evil the wind, and bitter the sea, and grey the sky,
> grey grey grey. (CPP 243)

which could well become strained and tedious if the chorus indulged in too much of it, changes to shorter and more mundane passages:

> One year the apples are abundant,
> Another year the plums are lacking.
> Yet we have gone on living,
> Living and partly living. (CPP 244)

Elsewhere the two functions of the Women, expressing both common human experience and also sensitivity to supernatural pressures, are united in the same speech, the balance shifting from one to another in successive lines or phrases:

> The New Year waits, breathes, waits, whispers in
> darkness.
> While the labourer kicks off a muddy boot and
> stretches his hand to the fire,
> The New Year waits, destiny waits for the coming.
> Who has stretched out his hand to the fire and
> remembered the Saints at All Hallows. (CPP 239)

In another way, the lyrical opening of the second part invests simple questions and answers with a weight of symbolic meaning:

> Does the bird sing in the south?
> Only the sea-bird cries, driven inland by the storm,
> What sign of the spring of the year?
> Only the sign of the old: not a stir, not a shoot, not a
> breath.
> Do the days begin to lengthen?
> Longer and darker the day, shorter and colder the
> night. (CPP 263)

Though Eliot had concluded that 'the more voices you have in your choir, the simpler and more direct the vocabulary, the syntax and the content of your lines must be' (3VP 7), he did not, as as far as one can see, simplify these choral speeches: certainly many of the words used are straightforward enough, but their unusual collocation and poetic context would make them difficult to guess at if there were any indistinctness in the speaking. Choral speaking happened at that period to be a popular accomplishment: many courses, demonstrations and competitions were held all over the country. It is not practised much now, but the muffled chanting the term evokes for us is nothing like the careful orchestration that, at its best, it was given in the 1930s. In the first Canterbury production, the chorus did not chant their lines – Eliot had considered a Yeatsian 'intoning' but rejected it – they varied between unison speaking, individual speakers and small groups to give different tone colour. Ivor Brown fifteen years later referred unkindly to the early days of religious drama when a 'chorus of chanting bores' was considered essential, but that was not what audiences found here. Elsie Fogerty, an acknowledged expert in voice and choral speaking, trained the chorus for the festival and subsequent transfers, and took great pains to avoid and check any hint of chanting, as well as planning vocal effect of each choral speech in turn, where to move from full sound to two or three speaking together:

> The problem was to find the exact number of speakers needed for each phrase in the chorus, and very soon we realised that we were doing not strictly choral work – but orchestral work; each speaker had to be like an instrument, in harmony with the other voices

> during the ensemble passages, but repeating a recurring phrase in an individual tone – just as flute or horn would do in an orchestra: one such phrase, I still remember is the 'Living – and partly living' of the first chorus; we tried four voices before finding the one that could give – quite naturally – the strange discouraged hopelessness of that line. (EMB 84)

Only eight women formed the chorus here, which was first necessitated by the cramped conditions of the Canterbury chapter house, where they had to remain on stage throughout the action; in 1972 a chorus of seven was used even on the much larger Aldwych stage, and in both cases limited numbers helped the clarity of the unison passages. Critics praised the verse-speaking of Robert Speaight as Becket, and of the chorus, describing the choral speeches as both beautiful and meaningful – which must confirm their audibility.

The choral speeches display wider variations of metrical form than the rest of the dialogue, but although Eliot briefly summed up his verse style as based on 'the versification of *Everyman*', this does not do justice to the flexibility of his staple dialogue in *Murder in the Cathedral*. Some passages are reminiscent of mediaeval drama earlier than *Everyman*, as in Thomas's lines

> For my Lord I am now ready to die,
> That his Church may have peace and liberty
> (CPP 275)

It is almost formulaic, in that Thomas is saying what must be said to fulfil the pattern of true martyrdom, an effect underlined by the rhyme. Wisely Eliot has not kept to a rigid rhyme scheme in the play, but uses different kinds of rhyme for different purposes: usually clear rhymes stress the force of statements in arguments, while occasional half-rhymes and echoes, suggesting a concealed pattern, are characteristic of the tempters' more insidious speeches.

Another effect of Eliot's adopting this form is that the dialogue tends to be built up of separate, detached line units, rather than running on into flowing imitation of conversational speech. Again, this has the impression of a series of facts or truths being laid down, as is fitting to the pattern-like, ritual nature of the play. Thomas particularly is given to gnomic or epigrammatic one-liners, such as 'I have therefore only to make perfect my will' and 'And I am not in danger: only near to death' (CPP 271). Within this overall style, however, the individual tempters, for instance, have distinct speech styles: the frivolous character of the first appears in his weak line-endings:

> Here I have come, forgetting all acrimony,
> Hoping that your present gravity
> Will find excuse for my humble levity. (CPP 246)

The second tempter, a man of power, forces his language into fixed shapes, into curtailed half-lines, alliterative balance and strong rhymes:

> King commands. Chancellor rightly rules.
> This is a sentence not taught in the schools.
> (CPP 249)

Dramatically, Eliot's verse accommodates the rising conflict as Thomas and tempter toss back and forth half-line questions and answers:

THOMAS: What shall we give for it?
TEMPTER: Pretence of priestly power.

culminating in the repeated, crashing 'No!' 'Yes!' (CPP 249) as argument gives way to the simple battle of opposed wills. The third tempter, anticlimactic in form as in content after this, has the short sentences of the country baron he claims to be, while the fourth tempter, by contrast, circles round Thomas politely:

> I offer what you desire, I ask
> What you have to give. Is it too much
> For such a vision of eternal grandeur? (CPP 255)

Because Thomas has already half-agreed with this tempter's ideas, the audience sees him here transformed into the victim instead of the victor of the temptation conflict. The intimate tone, the familiar 'Thomas', are insidious: subtle echoes and reminders are part of the tempter's armoury – note how he probes Thomas's love–hate relationship with Henry by the repetition of the world 'king' in his first three long speeches. His last, most disorienting stroke is to quote exactly Thomas's earlier words to the Women: 'You know and do not know, what it is to act or suffer' (CPP 255). Was his earlier assumption of understanding another snare, a sign of the sin of pride? He is not above the pattern, but like the Women must subdue himself to it.

Murder in the Cathedral is a play which succeeds more reliably in performance than Eliot's other plays, and one reason is the virtuoso range of verbal styles that he allowed himself, through all the variations of dialogue and including the extremes of choral lyricism and the ironically recognisable prose of the Knights. His management of these resources is bold and successful. Martin Browne recalls for instance the powerful effect of the abrupt change from the murder and the chorus's 'wash the brain, wash the soul, wash them, wash them' to the Knights' urbane and persuasive words, in the early performances at Canterbury, and also adds that a French production in translation, which could not reproduce the clichés and their humorous effect, gained in recompense a menacing seriousness that greatly impressed the author.

This first production was both a critical and a financial success: it moved to the small Mercury Theatre under the management of Ashley Dukes, Robert Speaight continuing as Becket, with other professional actors replacing the amateurs in the lesser roles. Here it ran for a year, with a brief excursion to Oxford and Cambridge, then transferred to the Duchess theatre in the West End. Interestingly, the play was televised live on 21 December 1936. It became something of a movable feast, touring the provinces where it attracted a new audience, returning to London briefly before going to America. A post-war revival was followed by a 1953 production with Robert Donat, then Richard Pascoe played Becket in 1972 at the Aldwych with the Royal Shakespeare Company. Proving how effective the play still was, this production balanced a primitive, physically assertive chorus with a powerful Christian typology in the martyrdom when, for instance, a cruciform pattern of light shone up through the stone-flagged stage as Becket lay dead.

Murder in the Cathedral also was made into a film, though this was not because it seemed an instantly popular story ripe for exploitation. The film director George Hoellering was experimenting with making films from poetic works, and initially thought of the original as a 'dramatic poem' rather than a finished realisation to be transferred from stage to screen. Eliot made some changes in the text because of the different demands of the film: he saw film as being more narrative, and the film audience as being more passive and needing more visual spelling-out of the situations than the stage audience. Hence he wrote in an introductory sequence involving Henry II and the initial conflict between him and Becket (noting that the inclusion of another strong figure would have spoilt the unified structure of the play). Obviously the film was able to use more varied locations, such as other parts of the cathedral, not just the chapter house, and the chorus was shown going about the normal daily work of mediaeval women. This freedom was used with restraint: Eliot praised Hoellering for cutting out some effective visual shots which would have distracted audiences from the accompanying spoken lines, but there was no way to keep in the direct address to the audience from the Knights – film could give the immediacy of the characters' experience, but not immediacy of contact with the actors. Eliot was interested in the implications of the distinction between the powers of film and stage:

> The first and most obvious difference, I found, was that the cinema (even where fantasy in introduced), is much more realistic than the stage. Especially in an historical picture, the setting, the costume, and the way of life represented have to be accurate. In watching a stage performance the member of the audience is in direct contact with the actor, is always conscious that he is looking at a stage and listening to an actor playing a part. . . . The difference between stage and screen in respect of realism is so great, I think, as to be a difference of kind rather than degree.[4]

This reinforces what Eliot already knew about the conventions of drama, but his wish to imitate life, to create the 'illusion of reality' was to supervene more and more from this point.

Why was *Murder in the Cathedral* such a significant play? The basic situation, the feelings of a man facing violent death, has a universal force, and the rest of the credit must go to Eliot's sudden achievement of dramatic skill in structure, dialogue and characterisation in making this potentially powerful subject into a satisfying whole; it is easy enough for the less skilful dramatist to let the same material degenerate into a melodramatic bloodbath or a static, monotonous welter of introspection. Here Eliot seemed to have achieved all his aims at once – the effective and non-derivative verse, the forceful message about the need for supernatural values even at the cost of life itself, accessibility to wider audiences, the relation both emotionally and explicitly to modern life, the strong plot, gripping action, balanced structure – with no more 'prentice work than *The Rock* behind him, Eliot's success was immediate and masterly.

However, he was not happy with his work, and spent the rest of his dramatic career in eliminating most of these qualities in pursuit of others. Somehow he seems to have felt that the virtues of *Murder in the Cathedral* did not count because it was a special case, and in his long post-mortem on the play he explains away all its merits: the audience's pleasure in his verse was merely due to its being 'about some remote historical period, far enough away from the present for the characters not to need to be recognisable as human beings, and therefore for them to be licensed to talk in verse. Picturesque period costume renders verse much more acceptable' (SP 76); his use of something like 'the verse of *Everyman*' as an alternative to hackneyed blank verse had been useful in suggesting historical period without archaism, but 'provided me with no clue to the verse I should use in another kind of play' (SP 77). The relevance of the chorus he rejected as a novice's prop; and the direct address to the audience by the knights was of dubious legitimacy:

> each transition makes the auditor aware, with a jolt, of the medium. It is, we may say, justifiable when the author wishes to produce this jolt: when he wishes to transport the audience violently from one plane of reality to another. (SP 69)

The Knights' speech fulfils his own criteria here for the rare admissibility of prose mixed with verse, but 'this is a kind of trick: that is, a device tolerably only in one play and of no use for any other' (SP 78–9). Thus, discarding both chorus and direct address as ways of relating the audience to the play, Eliot preferred to take the method of relating to contemporary life by imitating it:

> I was determined, therefore, in my next play to take a theme of contemporary life, with characters of our own time living in our own world. *The Family Reunion* was the result. (SP 79)

5
Later Eliot: 'The Family Reunion', 'The Cocktail Party' and the Other Modern Plays

Eliot's mission to increase the level of poetic awareness of audiences led to his seeking to conquer the fashionable West End theatrical establishment from within. There were to be no special allowances made for a worthy message or cultural snobbery – poetic drama should be able to compete with the commercial comedy or problem play at every level and win on its merits. He wanted to 'bring poetry into the world in which the audience lives and to which it returns when it leaves the theatre' (SP 79). So his next four plays were set in contemporary middle-class England. The language also differed from that of *Murder in the Cathedral*, moving more in the direction of 'ordinary colloquial speech'. All this meant that his modern plays were less radical and innovatory than *Murder*, and though he had called for a 'revolution in principles' for the theatre, his own work got progressively less revolutionary. In practice, the boldness of 'only by going too far can we find out how far we can go' (SP 64) is not really bold, because the underlying assumption is that the danger must lie in going too far –

Auden and Isherwood's *The Dog Beneath the Skin* at the Westminster Theatre (1936).

Alec Guinnes (left) in Auden and Isherwood's *The Ascent of F6.* Old Vic production (1939).

Robert Speaight as Beckett in the first production of Eliot's *Murder in the Cathedral* (1935).

Canterbury Cathedral Chapter House, setting for *Murder in the Cathedral* (1935).

Beckett and the four tempters in *Murder in the Cathedral* (1935).

Richard Pasco as Beckett in the Royal Shakespeare Company production of *Murder in the Cathedral* (1972).

Alec Clunes in Fry's *The Lady's Not For Burning*, original Arts Theatre production, (1948).

Stanley Baker, Leonard White and Denholm Elliot in Fry's *A Sleep of Prisoners*, (1951).

rather than, as one regretfully feels sometimes with Eliot, in not going far enough.

Three themes recur in Eliot's thinking about his plays: the special truth (the supernatural element) that he wanted to convey; the necessity of poetry as the means of best communicating that truth; and its acceptable communication to a wide audience. Probably any two of these would have been very significantly easier to combine than all three, and the problem of audience acceptability in particular progressively modified his views and his practice. Eliot's definition of poetry as opposed to 'merely verse' was: 'the language at those dramatic moments when it reaches intensity' (3VP 9) – if there was no intensity, there could be no poetry.

On this basis, there would be separate categories of (a) poetic situations requiring poetic language, and (b) non-poetic situations requiring non-poetic language. This is consistent with Eliot's principle that 'the music of poetry is not something which exists apart from the meaning' (SP 56), and leads to his rejection of poetry when used as 'merely a decoration'. Indeed, by this theory, adding poetry to a non-poetic situation would be not only undesirable but by definition impossible, because the intensity would not be there. Believing that 'a mixture of prose and verse in the same play is generally to be avoided', Eliot logically aimed at 'a form of verse in which everything can be said that has to be said' even though this all-purpose verse 'will only be "poetry" when the dramatic situation has reached such a point of intensity that poetry becomes the natural utterance' (SP 70). This is a more limiting definition of poetry than most people, then as now, would find acceptable, but even so the problem of making even occasional passages of intense poetry effective bedevilled his modern plays.

Eliot saw some of his difficulties and inconsistencies as temporary, and as being due to the experimental and transitional nature of his plays, and he looked forward to a time when he would 'dare to make liberal use of poetry and take greater liberties with ordinary colloquial speech'. This would happen when he had learnt to 'adapt it to the needs of the stage' and 'when (and if) the understanding of theatrical technique has become second nature' (SP 84). Some of his anxieties concern the management of the theatre audience – 'the unknown audience cannot be expected to show any indulgence toward the poet' (SP 76). Eliot's image of the audience as indifferent, potentially hostile and as something to be moulded, derives from his theatrical insecurity. Apart from his lack of professional theatrical experience, he was in an exposed position because he had no established convention to work with. Like the other modern poetic dramatists, he was starting afresh, and was theorising about what new conventions would be acceptable, with neither traditional nor instinctive guidance to an audience's reactions. Nonetheless, he had triumphed with *Murder in the Cathedral*, and had been encouraged by its success to begin another play, this time without the support of a commission.

If Becket is a man who returns home expecting to be killed and is killed, *The Family Reunion* (1939) is about a man in the reverse situation: Harry (Lord Monchensey) comes home thinking he has killed his wife, when apparently he has not. This is an even more 'limited action' than *Murder in the Cathedral*, though we are never absolutely sure whether Harry had pushed his wife off the liner (or did she fall, or did she jump?). Even the reunion of the title is not as expected, for Harry's younger brothers John and Arthur fail to arrive, though they also just fail to meet sudden deaths in collision with stationary objects. All this negative action meant some bafflement for audiences, as Harry's return home for his widowed, dominating mother's birthday is, in short, a mysterious event. Amy, his mother, and his obtuse uncles and aunts are half-incredulous, half-panicky at his distraught claims to have killed his unsuitable wife. Only his aunt Agatha and his second cousin Mary see his anguish as part not of a 'nervous breakdown' but of a productive spiritual crisis, a transition from seeing the world as a hopeless wasteland, 'shrieking forms in a circular desert' (CPP 335), to entering a world of spiritual values, where 'safety and danger have a different meaning' (CPP 342). Harry is pursued not by tempters or assassins, but by the Furies themselves, the supernatural Eumenides who appear at intervals to him and to us.

At first Harry thinks of them as avengers of his dead wife, but later they fulfil the literal, propitiatory meaning of their Greek name, the Kindly Ones, and personify his spiritual challenge. This is Eliot's recurrent theme, the problem of finding a meaningful pattern behind the sick materialism of the world. With the help of Agatha and Mary, Harry recognises his crisis for what it is, and against his mother's wishes he leaves again, this time not fleeing but seeking his salvation. From his attempts to elucidate the whole intangible process, Amy deduces that he is going to become a missionary. 'I never said that I was going to be a missionary' (CPP 344) cries poor Harry, who naturally cannot explain simply a situation that Eliot had taken care to present as unclear, irrational and subject to non-material standards. Nonetheless, he departs, and Amy goes into the next room where she dies, as she has feared, alone.

Harry's insight is provoked by Agatha's account of

how she and his father long ago fell in love and how his father had planned to murder his mother, then pregnant with Harry. There are echoes here of the doctrine of original sin, so that Harry is like Thomas in having to fulfil a pattern, to expiate a burden of guilt not specifically his own. But although it is suggested that 'You are the consciousness of your unhappy family' (CPP 333) and Harry's own repetition of 'until I come again' has a messianic ring, he is far less aware of what is at stake or of what pattern he is involved in than Thomas was. Like all the later protagonists, Harry is for most of the play foundering in the confusion of a pre-religious state of mind. In his case, this leads to preoccupation with his own experience of desolation, and impatience with the concerns of everyone else or indeed of their attempts to understand him; and he is rather inclined to lecture the others on this:

> What I'm telling you
> Is very important. Very important.
> You must let me explain, and then you can
> talk. (CPP 318)
>
> What you call the normal
> Is merely the unreal and the unimportant.
> I was like that in a way. (CPP 326)

While his obsession with his own spiritual crisis is understandable, it makes his behaviour towards the 'normal' characters unpleasantly callous and cavalier, and Eliot later commented 'my hero now strikes me as an insufferable prig' (SP 82). The problem is that Eliot has not successfully aligned the two levels of significance in his play, so that the same event can be serious on both levels at once – a problem he solves noticeably better in *The Cocktail Party*. So here in stressing the profound effect which the death of his wife, and the reported attempted murder by his father have on Harry's view of life, Eliot mistakenly dismisses the natural human reaction to these as comparatively unimportant. This similarly afflicts the role of Agatha, already a thankless part for an actress, being almost entirely composed of aphorisms, advice and other generalisations. Only when she describes and analyses the past, and recalls her own past experience does her authority gain substance, and the sybilline voice becomes human:

> There are hours when there seems to be no past or
> future,
> Only a present moment of pointed light
> When you want to burn. When you stretch out your
> hand
> To the flames. They only come once,
> Thank God, that kind. Perhaps there is another kind,
> I believe, across a whole Thibet of broken stones
> That lie, fang up, a lifetime's march. I have believed
> this. (CPP 332)

And then humanity is shattered by her casual reaction to Harry's responsibility for his wife's death: 'Perhaps I only dreamt I pushed her' suggests Harry, and Agatha replies briskly

> So I had supposed. What of it?
> What we have written is not a story of detection,
> Of crime and punishment, but of sin and expiation.
> (CPP 333)

The 'What of it?' implies not that sin is more important than crime, but that sin is important and crime is not, and the audience is unlikely to feel happy about this.

As the appearance of the Eumenides (rather than of some more domestic ghost) suggests, Eliot is basing this modern action on the framework of Greek mythology. Harry has been compared with Orestes, the son of Agamemnon doomed to avenge his father's death by killing his mother, but the similarity is rather in the general sense of accursedness and the pressure of the Furies than in detail – wife-murder is more a preoccupation of Eliot than of Greek tragedy, which gives tragic stature to the murder of husbands and fathers, and, at a pinch, mothers, but not wives. What in Christian terms is a burden of sin, at another level seems to be a curse, where Harry is re-enacting his father's willed though not achieved murder. As in *Murder in the Cathedral*, there is a reminder of the ritual needs of disturbed humanity: ritual acknowledges the sense of guilt, expiates the curse, averts evil, or lays spirits to rest. This is seen not only in the appearance of the Furies to Harry but in the incantation-like lines of Harry and Agatha: 'Over and under . . . In and out' suggesting that certain actions must go on being repeated to fulfil a curse, while the ritual of Mary and Agatha around Amy's birthday cake marks the end of that curse.

Eliot himself came to feel more sympathetic towards the less elevated characters of Amy and the chauffeur Downing. Amy is an interesting and rounded character, her will power and complaints being based as we learn from Agatha on a life of disappointment and deprival. Her bitterness at the loss of what she has cherished as her last hope is affecting, once the suffering and endurance of her marriage are known. The confrontations between her and Agatha take on an Ibsenesque power and tension, even though they are not speaking in the same terms.

The chauffeur on the other hand is, like some of the builders in *The Rock*, rather too good and perceptive to be true. A forerunner of Eggerson in *The Confidential Clerk*, he is instinct with natural benevolence, wisdom, loving kindness and insight deeper than anyone else's. Downing may be humane, but he is not as human as the uncles and aunts whose bickerings and jealousies make them more convincingly rounded. Eliot in fact also valued Uncle Charles highly – he is the one who has glimpses of what Harry is trying to convey – 'there is something I *could* understand, if I were told it' (CPP 345). He echoes Sweeney's 'Any man might do a girl in' with

> I might have done the same thing once, myself,
> Nobody knows what he's likely to do
> Until there's somebody he wants to get rid of.
> (CPP 297)

His less conventional reaction to Harry's confession hints at his ability to reach beyond the material level:

> I thought that life could bring no further surprises;
> But I remember now, that I am always surprised
> By the bulldog in the Burlington Arcade.
> What if every moment were like that, if one were
> awake? (CPP 346)

Eliot wrote to Browne that Charles was saved by this capacity for surprise, and was the character 'most like myself' (EMB 106).

The use of the need to 'do a girl in' is probably a

distracting remnant of Eliot's earlier attempts at playwriting, brought in as a useful focus for Harry's feelings of disorientation. Hugh Kenner comments on Eliot's liking for this motif: 'Throughout *The Wasteland*, in *Sweeney Agonistes*, and in *The Family Reunion*, Prufrock disguised as Sweeney and as Harry, drowned this woman over and over'[1] and he adds that *The Family Reunion* is 'a rewriting of *Sweeney Agonistes*'. Rewriting is a large term for the relationship between two fragments and a full-length play, but *The Family Reunion* fulfils better Eliot's earlier intention to write about a more sensitive character whose language is understood by the audience but not by most of the other less sensitive characters on stage. Harry's sensitivity may seem selective, but he struggles hard to overcome the problem of communication, realising the incomprehension of the other characters: Sweeney's baffled 'I gotta use words when I talk to you' corresponds to Harry's

I talk in general terms
Because the particular has no language.
(CPP 294)

and

that's not the language
I choose to be talking. I will not talk yours. (CPP 324)

and

Oh, there *must* be another way of talking
That would get us somewhere. (CPP 327)

So Harry strives to present his deeply disturbed feelings to his family in terms of mundane objects, invoking the 'noxious smell' and the 'unspoken voice of sorrow in the ancient bedroom' (CPP 294). Only when Agatha recommends him to 'Talk in your own language' does he move to more typical Eliotian wasteland symbolism, which is probably recognisable and comprehensible at least to followers of Eliot the poet among the audience, though still not meaningful to Harry's family. His state of mind has been one of desolation for a long period:

> The sudden solitude in a crowded desert
> In a thick smoke, many creatures moving
> Without direction, for no direction
> Leads anywhere but round and round in that vapour –
> Without purpose, and without principle of conduct
> In flickering intervals of light and darkness;
> The partial anaesthesia of suffering without feeling
> And partial observation of one's own automatism
> While the slow stain sinks deeper through the skin
> Tainting the flesh and discolouring the bone –
> This is what matters, but it is unspeakable,
> Untranslatable. (CPP 294)

Like the Women of Canterbury, he has come to see all life as absurd, sickening, meaningless. He later tells Agatha that this began eight years previously, about the time he left Wishwood, but it seems not merely a product of his marriage – rather the marriage has brought home to him the horror of any existence that is 'Without purpose, and without principle of conduct'. Learning of his father's intentions of murder, the real cause of the hostility, oppression and mystery that had shrouded his childhood, Harry cries 'Everything is true in a different sense' – even a horrific meaning is better than meaninglessness. Now the desert image becomes a sign of cleanliness, pilgrimage and purgation:

> Somewhere on the other side of despair.
> To the worship in the desert, the thirst and deprivation,
> A stony sanctury and a primitive altar,
> The heart of the sun and the icy vigil,
> A care over lives of humble people,
> The lesson of ignorance, of incurable diseases.
> (CPP 339)

Amy, taking this for a real desert, makes her 'missionary' deduction – she is still not understanding the language Harry speaks.

Only Harry and Agatha really communicate at all levels, expressing their intense misery by separate chains of images in a dialogue in which both follow their own trains of thought, matching without answering the other's parallel lamentation. Agatha begins with Eliot's recurrent image of the unreachable, Alice in Wonderland rose garden through a little door, then is condemned to walk away:

> And then I was only my own feet walking
> Away down a concrete corridor . . .
> I was only the feet, and the eye
> Seeing the feet: the unwinking eye
> Fixing the movement. Over and under. (CPP 335)

For his part, Harry is still imprisoned in his Dantesque wilderness:

> In and out, in an endless drift
> Of shrieking forms in a circular desert
> Weaving with contagion of putrescent embraces
> On dissolving bone. (CPP 335)

Communication is confirmed at the end when Harry suggests his hopes in terms of Agatha's imagery

> I was not there, you were not there, only our phantasms
> And what did not happen is as true as what did happen
> O my dear, and you walked through the little door
> And I ran to meet you in the rose-garden. (CPP 335)

But Agatha replies that 'We do not pass twice through the same door' – his new understanding is a new beginning, not the happy ending.

This kind of communication, where elusive shades of meaning, the 'frontiers' of consciousness beyond which words fail', are compressed into symbol and image, is only one strand of Eliot's writing in the play. Important dialogue of a more functional kind is muscular and effective: Amy's first speech, as she stops the maid from drawing the curtains, with evident symbolism, 'Not yet! I will ring for you. It is still quite light.' is as peremptory as we are to find her in the rest of the play, with the defiance suggesting her misgivings, soon expressed in a more Chekhovian, less naturalistic reverie

> O Sun, that was once so warm, O Light that was taken
>   for granted
> When I was young and strong, and sun and light
>   unsought for
> And the night unfeared and the day expected
> And clocks could be trusted, tomorrow assured
> And time would not stop in the dark! (CPP 285)

while her more limited sister Ivy cuts in with Sweeney-like repetitions

I have always told Amy she should go south in the
winter.
Were I in Amy's position, I would go south in the winter
I would follow the sun, not wait for the sun to come
here.
I would go south in the winter, if I could afford it.
(CPP 285)

Eliot thought that he had in some ways improved on *Murder in the Cathedral* here: his line of variable length with three stresses, any number of weak syllables and a caesura gave him 'a rhythm close to contemporary speech, in which the stresses could be made to come where ever we should naturally put them' (SP 80). But there were already signs of the conflict between naturalness and poetry that was to disturb his playwriting. Certain poetic passages of dialogue do not rise smoothly from the 'ordinary' verse but have a definite awkwardness in performance. One of these occurs where Mary reasons convincingly with Harry that, even in his own terms, the 'unreality' of life at Wishwood must cast doubts also on the 'reality' of his despair and disgust – his own subjective impressions are no guarantee on the validity of one or the other. From this argument, Mary and Harry go on to a lyrical dialogue too allusive and self-contained to fit in with any kind of realism.

HARRY: Perhaps you are right, though I do not know
How you should know it. Is the cold spring
Is the spring not an evil time, that excites us with
lying voices?
MARY: The cold spring now is the time
For the ache in the moving root
The agony in the dark . . .

HARRY: Spring is an issue of blood
A season of sacrifice
And the wail of the new full tide
Returning the ghosts of the dead. (CPP 310)

This again is the language of 'The Waste Land', and Harry wrenches it back to 'natural' dialogue with 'What have we been saying? I think I was saying . . .' The same deliberate change of gear occurs when the characters have to behave symbolically and non-realistically, as well as departing from conversational speech, as when Agatha after the second appearance of the Eumenides, goes 'in somnambular fashion' to stand where they had stood and voices the hidden meaning of their presence and Harry's past:

A curse comes to being
As a child is formed. (CPP 336)

and concludes 'What have I been saying? I think I was saying . . .' This is surely akin to the 'jolt' between two planes of reality which Eliot had decided not to repeat after its successful use for the Knight's speech in *Murder in the Cathedral*. Its appearance here suggests that it *has* its uses, but that Eliot is still not accepting it, is trying to conceal the 'jolt' by apologising for it – which of course does not conceal it at all but on the contrary draws the audience's attention to the inconsistency of style in a negative way. Because the characters sound embarrassed at what the playwright has made them do, Eliot falls as it were between two stools and neither jolts the audience positively nor retains the illusion of reality.

Eliot handles other ritualised passages with more assurance, as in Agatha's first exposition of the 'curse', when she comes on to an empty stage, speaks her lines, then leaves, with no need for transition or reference to other characters; the final sequence of the play consists of Agatha's and Mary's ritual invocations or prayers, while they walk round and round the dead Amy's birthday cake, blowing out the candles until there is darkness:

> Round and round the circle
> Completing the charm
> So the knot be unknotted
> The crossed be uncrossed
> The crooked be made straight
> And the curse be ended. (CPP 350)

However, it is doubtful whether his more assured approach makes these episodes fully acceptable, simply because of the mixture of associations brought in. References to bones in a well, weasel and otter, to a curse, and to a 'charm', have overtones of 'Eye of newt and toe of frog', confusing to an audience struggling to penetrate to an experience beyond the ordinary powers of communication, an experience already borrowing symbols from the Christian and ancient Greek religious repertoire. Evidently Agatha and Mary have a role as spokeswomen for the forces driving Harry, but how this supplements their natural wisdom and why it takes this not quite appropriate Black Magic form, is a distracting aspect of the play.

This is one of the features that can be pinpointed as transitional between the poetic convention of *Murder*, and the increasing realism of the later plays; Eliot did not wish to eliminate poetic commentary from above or outside the action, and so had to distribute it among his characters. He felt then that 'I had, indeed, made some progress in dispensing with the chorus'. But he was still highly self-critical. The chorus-substitute, whereby the four lesser uncles and aunts take on a choral function to voice common and unconscious feelings about the situation, expressing significance they are not as individuals aware of, was 'not very satisfactory'. Like the Knights' address to the audience, this sort of breaking of the illusion is common in modern plays, but to Eliot 'It seemed to me another trick' (SP 80). The same misgivings are felt about the Furies:

> We tried every possible manner of presenting them. We put them on the stage and they looked like uninvited guests who had strayed in from a fancy-dress ball. We concealed them behind gauze, and they suggested a still out of a Walt Disney film. We made them dimmer, and they looked like shrubbery just outside the window. I have seen other expedients tried: I have seen them signalling from across the garden, or swarming on to the stage like a football team, and they are never right.

He decided therefore that 'They must in future be omitted from the cast, and be understood to be visible only to certain of my characters, and not to the audience' (SP 82).

With the chorus, E. Martin Browne agreed that the 'trick' aspect did not suit the play: originally he like other directors marked the change of convention by some method, but later felt that this was wrong: the play 'should be taken at its own face value' (EMB 127), that is, the choral speeches should be offered unobtrusively and naturalistically. Modern productions, however, do tend to mark choruses and keep in the Furies. Katharine

Worth wondered how far Eliot's 'curious judgements spring from experience of inadequate productions, how far from the need under which he seems to have laboured, to apologise for, or turn away from, what is most alive and disturbing in his dramatic experiments' and goes on to describe Michael Eliot's 1966 production in the round with a student cast.

> He successfully disregarded Eliot's injunction against making the Furies visible, contriving with the aid of beautifully controlled modulations of light into darkness, spectacular incarnations for them as towering black shapes, alarmingly materialising between the audience who saw round a skeletal framework enclosing the haunted room, and the characters. Harry made his entrance through the room where the audience sat, pausing with them for a long look at the family exposed to view a few yards away in the lighted framework before stepping into it and exchanging the watcher's role for the actor's. . . . This physical involvement of the audience in Harry's experience was completed when the Eumenides materialised between him and them, overlooking both, forcing them out of their safe role as watchers.[2]

In 1979 Michael Eliot did another production, this one professional, which began in the round in Manchester, though it transferred to a proscenium stage in the London West End Vaudeville theatre, and there again the Eumenides were towering figures that suddenly and compellingly appeared, this time with electronic sound as well as lighting effects. The shattering impact on the audience was quite different from the limp puzzlement that Eliot's comments suggest. Michael Eliot agreed with E. Martin Browne that the play should mainly be anchored in the very realistic world, but only as a basis for insisting on an equally present alternative extraordinary world: 'two worlds that interleave and flow through each other, simultaneous and yet apart, which are the product of fantasy, hallucination, of something closer to mysticism'.[3]

The original production of *The Family Reunion* met with some bafflement from critics and audiences as to its theme, quite apart from the reactions to the Eumenides and the chorus of uncles and aunts. It had opened in March 1939 in the increasingly fraught atmosphere before Britain entered the Second World War, and the Westminster theatre management which had agreed to take it had at this time a policy of putting on plays of high artistic and intellectual quality but for short limited runs. Even so, a run of only five weeks for *The Family Reunion* must have been a disappointment for Eliot, and perhaps was one factor in his not beginning another play until 1948. Michael Redgrave played Harry, and is said to have asked Eliot where Harry really did go after the end of the play, if he was not in fact going to be a missionary, and Eliot told him that Harry and the chauffeur Downing both go off to work in the East End of London. When the play was revived by Martin Browne after the war at the Mercury theatre in 1946 and at the Edinburgh Festival in 1947, reviews explicitly stated their acceptance of the choral convention, but hazarded only a general interpretation of curse and expiation, and had still little to suggest on how the different parts of the plot fitted into this interpretation.

The changes of level for chorus and Eumenides then have become more acceptable with time; the continuing problem is what exactly happens to Harry during the play (rather than afterwards). He arrives, he is full of *weltschmerz*, he hears that his father once planned to kill his mother, and all at once he is reconciled and purposeful. To some extent this is sound psychology; like the Women of Canterbury he cannot cope with the sinister and inexplicable atmosphere and attitudes of his background. Once a reason is given, then the causes and effects become clear, if tragic, and he feels there is a possibility of acting for good and striving for meaning. But the process takes place in some obscurity and the plot element does not – perhaps because of its remoteness in time – really measure up to the immediacy and power of the effect on Harry. Similarly Agatha's suggestion that 'You are the consciousness of your unhappy family' (CPP 333), given their lack of participation in his experience, is very hard to sustain on any level. In a letter to Martin Browne, Eliot explained:

> At the beginning of the play he is aware of the past only as *pollution* and he does not dissociate the pollution of his wife's life from that of her death. He still wants to *forget*, and that is the way forbidden. (It is not I who have forbidden it, I see it as Law.) Only after the second visit of the Furies does he begin to understand what the Way of Liberation is: and he follows the Furies as immediately and as unintelligibly as the Disciples dropping their nets. (EMB 108)

Harry is to be liberated from the sins of his own and his family's past by doing good and being good, but many contemporary reviews, while approving the poetry, still found the significance far from clear: Eliot was to unite plot and significance much more closely in *The Cocktail Party*.

In comparison with the serious and obscure *The Family Reunion*, *The Cocktail Party* (1949) effectively spells out three, possibly four, spiritual transitions, with its sense of humour intact. So far Eliot was right in believing he had avoided 'some of the errors' of his previous play (though solemnity was not what he meant). In retrospect he had come to prefer Amy to Harry, because the latter seemed a prig: the choice of comedy for the new play was one way of guarding against priggishness. He seems to have first had the idea of one element of his double plot, the failing marriage of Edward and Lavinia. The opening situation is that Lavinia has unexpectedly left Edward on the eve of a cocktail party: and though it turns out that Lavinia had known that Edward was having an affair with Celia, he had not known that she was having an affair with Peter. Perhaps over-symmetrically, Eliot has made Peter fall out of love with Lavinia and into love with Celia. This is more reminiscent of Noel Coward's *Private Lives* than Euripides, but Eliot explained:

> I was still inclined to go to a Greek dramatist for my theme, but I was determined to do so merely as a point of departure, and to conceal the origins so well that nobody would identify them until I pointed them out myself. In this at least I have been successful; for no one of my acquaintance (and no dramatic critics) recognized the source of my story in the *Alcestis* of Euripides. (SP 83)

The disappearing wife is the only common point of the two plays; in *Alcestis* she is brought back from the dead by the demigod hero Hercules, while Lavinia is brought back for an attempt at reconciliation by the 'great doctor' – evidently a psychiatrist of some kind – Sir

Henry Harcourt-Reilly. Eliot had been interested in what kind of life would be possible for a couple one of whom had sacrificed herself and been resurrected: Edward and Lavinia are far more disunited than their Greek originals, and this crisis forces them to face the basic question of what is wrong with themselves and their lives.

However, their problems are soon overshadowed by the predicament of Celia, whose rejection by Edward just when she expects him to take advantage of Lavinia's disappearance to marry her, shocks her into clear-eyed dismay at what a life without illusions actually is. Her shock is not as apocalyptic as Harry's 'murder', perhaps, but it equally leaves her in a state of confused despair until she can find a meaning and a direction for her life. Again Sir Henry comes to the rescue, and directs her to his 'sanatorium' where spiritual guidance will be available. Two years later, the last act shows Edward and Lavinia reconciled and adjusted but not complacent, and at a repeat cocktail party, they learn of Celia's death. She had gone as a nursing sister of an 'austere order' to a tropical country where an uprising has resulted in her being crucified beside an ant hill. Amid the horror, regret and guilt of those who had lost interest in her, Peter is the only character who has kept the hope of encountering her again; this shock is perhaps a turning point for him, as he rather hastily rejects, then accepts his career as a film script writer.

Eliot had initially decided 'no chorus, and no ghosts' but he has three 'aware' characters – Sir Henry himself, and two other old friends of those involved, Julia and Alex – who are 'Guardians' in the play: they nudge the struggling characters on the way they ought to go, understand their plight and comment on the action in the light of a context of other struggles. Their comments then have a kind of choral relationship to the action, though they do not themselves represent the general relevance of the main characters' experiences, as did the Women of Canterbury or Harry's uncles and aunts. Some critics objected to the interference of these superior outsiders, but the informed and evidently well-considered motives of the three are more acceptable than Agatha's individual pontificating. Edward and Lavinia themselves are representative rather than exceptional characters. They typify the superior kind of modern furnished flat people, being of a better class but just as devoid of values and convictions as Sweeney's friends. Edward confesses to Sir Henry, at first unknown to him except as an uninvited guest at the party – because 'it's easier to talk to a person you don't know' – that he needs Lavinia back to 'find out who she is, to find out who I am' (CPP 364). Sir Henry agrees: 'There's a loss of personality' and goes on 'You are nothing but a set of obsolete responses' (CPP 363). His role of permanent opposition to Lavinia has gone, and without her he 'dissolves'. In this play the characters become more and more isolated as their worldly concerns are stripped away, including their reliance on human relationships. 'Are we all in fact unloving and unlovable? Then one *is* alone' (CPP 416) exclaims Celia, and Edward tells Lavinia

> What is hell? Hell is oneself,
> Hell is alone, the other figures in it
> Merely projections. There is nothing to escape from
> Any nothing to escape to. One is always alone. (CPP 39)

Martin Browne recalls Eliot turning to him as these lines were spoken and whispering 'Contre Sartre'

(EMB 233), referring to Sartre's dictum in *Huis Clos* that 'Hell is other people'. But Edward and Lavinia do, as in Sartre's philosophy, define themselves in terms of other people, absent or present; Edward cannot live without Lavinia who has 'made me incapable of having any existence of my own' (CPP 403) and Lavinia does not love anyone, but wants to be loved. All this is very clearly expressed, and to raise it above the mere psychological case study of *folie à deux*, Sir Henry simply has to insist, again very clearly, that their desolate state is permanent and part of the human condition. As they have found, other relationships make no difference. From their recognition of their situation, they can begin to build at least a tolerable life: they are to 'make the best of a bad job' with the hope that now they are 'stripped naked to their souls' they will be less likely to try to act selfishly under the disguise of self-righteousness.

This is the normal plight, but Celia, on the other hand, has Becket's role as the active asserter of spiritual values. Her recognition of desolation does not lead her to make the best of it, but to seek a spiritual satisfaction that will realise the feeling she thought she had for Edward. Sir Henry does not suggest what she is going to do, any definite programme risks sounding as banal as Harry's 'missionary' label, but the implication is that she has to renounce the everyday world altogether. The choices of all three have the common point that all are avoiding mere selfishness, self-deception and materialism, and Celia's example later encourages and reinforces the others.

The relationship of the two levels of action – what the characters do, and the significance it has – works well here, as it did in *Murder in the Cathedral*, but did not in *The Family Reunion*. However, Eliot was right to worry about the development of his dramatic language in this play:

> I laid down for myself the ascetic rule to avoid poetry which could not stand the test of strict dramatic utility: with such success, indeed, that it is perhaps an open question whether there is any poetry in the play at all. (SP 83)

The language of most of the characters is less incisive, because more realistic than in *The Family Reunion*. Celia is a particular culprit here. Her invocations of betrayal, atonement and a sense of sin are packaged in the space-filling, unmeaning turns of phrase of ordinary conversation 'I suppose . . . in fact, at least . . . it leaves me cold . . . you see' dilute her speeches. There are a few passages where her speech becomes more formal – the 'can'ts' become 'cannots' – and uses a greater range of reference and implication:

> I have thought at moments that the ecstasy is real
> Although those who experience it may have no reality.
> For what happened is remembered like a dream
> In which one is exalted by intensity of loving
> In the spirit, a vibration of delight
> Without desire, for desire is fulfilled
> In the delight of loving. (CPP 417)

Otherwise her speeches have a muffled quality because something is being expressed in an inappropriate and apologetic way. On the other hand the colloquialism of the party scene is complex and effective, in that language is being used both with irony and to comment on its own conventions. Julia for instance interrogates Edward who is desperately lying about an aunt he has invented as an excuse for Lavinia's absence:

> JULIA: I feel as if I knew
> All about that aunt in Hampshire.
> EDWARD: Hampshire?
> JULIA: Didn't you say Hampshire?
> EDWARD: No, I didn't say Hampshire.
> JULIA: Did you say Hampstead?
> EDWARD: No, I didn't say Hampstead.
> JULIA: But she must live somewhere.
> EDWARD: She lives in Essex.
> JULIA: Anywhere near Colchester? Lavinia loves oysters.
> EDWARD: No. In the *depths* of Essex.
> JULIA: Well, we won't probe into it.
> You have the address and the telephone number?
> (CPP 357)

By writing pauses into similarly repetitive question dialogue, Pinter gets the same effect of menacing advance and retreat as Eliot's repetition combined with verse rhythm achieves.

Sir Henry has the most flexible language, making, for instance a point about incongruity in two contrasting lines, one allusive, one simple:

> We talk of darkness, labyrinths, Minotaur terrors.
> But that world does not take the place of this one.
> (CPP 438)

He also has several portentous, Agatha-like lines, such as 'Disillusion can become itself an illusion/If we rest in it' (CPP 417). Martin Browne counted himself 'supremely lucky' in securing Alec Guinness for this part in the Edinburgh production, and he quotes Robert Speaight on the performance:

> The gesture with which Mr. Alec Guinness took out his watch on these last words was perhaps the most imaginative moment in a magnificent performance. Sir Henry might so easily have become an ethical bore, sugaring his pills with whimsy. But with Mr. Guinness we are worlds away from ethics; this is the confessional and the choice is between the loss of personality and the love of God. (EMB 237)

Edward too is given some telling passages where simplicity has great force in his self-analysis:

> The self that wills – he is a feeble creature;
> He has to come to terms in the end
> With the obstinate, the tougher self; who does not speak,
> Who never talks, who cannot argue;
> And how in some men may be the *guardian* –
> But in men like me, the dull, the implacable,
> The indomitable spirit of mediocrity. (CPP 381)

But because the simplicity is uniform everywhere in order to keep an illusion of realism, and occurs even in expressions of emotion, which Eliot would allow to become poetic, then even the poetry is prevented by this realistic simplicity from ever daring the original or unexpected. The form is that of ordinary syntax and vocabulary, instead of boldly inverting, listing, imaging, as in *Murder*. For instance, characteristic Eliotian repetition in this play is spread over normal sentence structure, so that it is tedious rather than assertive:

This is the worst moment, when you feel that you have
lost
The desire for all that was most desirable,
Before you are contented with what you can desire;
Before you know what is left to be desired;
And you go on wishing that you could desire
What desire has left behind. (CPP 381)

and there are more pedestrian lines still

CELIA: There was never anything
Between me and Peter.
EDWARD: Wasn't there?
He thought so. He came back this evening to talk to
me about it.
CELIA: But this is ridiculous. I never gave Peter
Any cause to suppose I cared for him. (CPP 380)

This is prose, and there is no reason why it should not be written as prose. The language of the play then succeeds when meaning dares to seek allusive expression, and when dialogue flaunts its own verbal felicity, as in Julia's speeches, but in between its status as verse hardly seems worth sustaining.

Sir Henry's is probably the dominant role in the play, though there are several clearly defined, large character parts, all of which, even the mysterious Alex and the late-developing Peter, have their own opportunities and set pieces, far more so than the often shadowy uncles and aunts in *The Family Reunion*. It is thus a candidate for the all-star cast type of production, which may have helped to maintain its popularity. In practice, such a production can impair the force of Edward and Lavinia as representative figures: if they are seen mainly as scintillating, witty sparring partners in the Coward tradition, they are eclipsed by Celia's tragic death, and their humbler parallel conversion passes unnoticed.

But the comic framework of secrets and different levels of meaning works well for Eliot, in that it blends into his manipulation of more serious levels of meaning at the climax of the play. The earlier comic situations arise because of the cocktail party itself, and the curiosity and benevolence of the guests clash incongruously and amusingly with the concealed marital crisis of Edward and Lavinia; Eliot shows considerable comic skills in the carefully built-up running joke of Julia's and Alex's repeated tactless interventions into Edward's conversations with Celia, Peter and the Unknown Guest. Later, the marital crisis becomes in turn the incongruous camouflage of a deeper spiritual crisis, more sympathetically handled here by Eliot than in *The Family Reunion*.

Nonetheless, if the comedy is overplayed, especially with the sort of naturalistic set that Eliot originally requested – typically for fear of getting 'late imitation of "experimental" theatre' – it will tend to conceal the depths of the characters' anguish. The director of a television adaptation, Michael Barry, chose a set which by use of walls and bar-like room dividers, suggested imprisonment. He also cut the text because with the intimate close-ups of the television camera, the viewer could 'perceive immediately the tremor of an eyelid on occasions when a speech might be required to carry the same meaning to the back of a theatre dress circle'.[4] Both imprisonment and the meaningful tremor are psychological interpretations of the situation, but Eliot is not giving what we would normally think of as psychological explanations – as Celia awkwardly puts it, her spiritual malaise resists the conventional labelling of 'bad form, or mental kinks' (CPP 415). Eliot is as usual not primarily concerned with psychology, and it is not for him an end or an explanation in itself, but a factor in the overriding pattern, a pattern which is like Yeats's tragic universality, though for Eliot the pattern cannot ultimately be called tragic as it leads to purpose and salvation without the overplus of tragic waste. This perhaps is what results in the accusation of a certain coldness in Eliot's picture: he rejects many human values along with materialism, setting value on what lies beyond – hence Agatha's dismissal of the dead wife, and Sir Henry's more qualified and sympathetic satisfaction at Celia's death:

> That way, which she accepted, led to this death.
> And if that is not a happy death, what death is happy?
> (CPP 437)

By this time, Eliot's reputation was such that Martin Browne had succeeded in finding him a distinguished cast and the support of the impresario Henry Sherek for *The Cocktail Party* which opened at the Edinburgh Festival in 1949 with very great success. Then, because of problems finding theatres in London, it went to New York where it was an even greater success, returning to London later while many of the original cast remained with the American production. It is a play which sustains different approaches: The 1962 Chichester revival of *The Cocktail Party* insisted on the brooding depths of the play, with Eileen Atkins as a fey, driven Celia, and Alec Guinness repeating his profound and dominating performance as Sir Henry, but in 1986 Alec McCowan developed a more emphatic, mobile interpretation of the part. A smaller but brisker figure, rapidly moving round the stage, while rapping out reprimands and sudden loud assertions, his Sir Henry was more human and less supernatural in his idiosyncrasies, and blended rather than conflicted with the restless modern Edward–Lavinia world to which John Dexter's colourful brittle production gave central thematic importance.

This was perhaps the peak of Eliot's popular success as a dramatist; the high box office returns show that audiences might claim to be baffled by the evident deeper meaning of the play but found enough entertainment and intriguing hints of hidden depths to keep interest high. Eliot's next play, *The Confidential Clerk*, did not seem to have either the same sparkle or the same depths, though it verges in places on the farcical, and possibly he was trying to overcorrect this with his more solemn last play, *The Elder Statesman*.

The Confidential Clerk (1953) is a more positive play than its predecessors, in that it not only ends on a note of reconciliation, but almost eliminates suffering from the whole body of the plot. No one dies, by sword, sea or ant hill, and critics compare it with Wilde's *The Importance of Being Earnest* because of the motif of the missing or mistaken child. This motif has a long and respectable ancestry, and David Jones[5] shows how closely Eliot's plot follows that of Euripides's *Ion*, only more so, for Eliot has three dubiously parented young people in play. Sir Claude and Lady Elizabeth Mulhammer have no legal children, though Sir Claude has an acknowledged illegitimate daughter Lucasta Angel, and Lady Elizabeth has had an illegitimate son, farmed out and lost in babyhood. Sir Claude's new confidential clerk, Colby, however, is introduced as yet another of his illegitimate children, newly informed of this fact, and it seems as though the main theme is going to be Lady Elizabeth's acceptance of him. However, as in any farce or Greek play, coincidence takes over by leaps and bounds, and Lady Elizabeth claims that the Mrs Guzzard who raised Colby is a name she remembers in connection with her own lost infant. Faced with Sir Claude's certainty, she hypothesises another child in Mrs Guzzard's care. Sir Claude protests 'You are suggesting that she ran a baby farm? That's not very likely, these days' (CPP 498) but in the last act an interview with Mrs Guzzard proves both Lady Elizabeth's memory and her hypothesis at least partially correct. There *were* two babies, but Lady Elizabeth's son grew up to be B. Kaghan, a brash young man who has somehow come to work for Sir Claude and whom she rather dislikes; and the other baby, Colby, is not Sir Claude's son either, but Mrs Guzzard's own legitimate child whom she has passed off as Sir Claude's (who died unborn when its mother died) for the money. Colby, who has thwarted ambitions to become a musician, now feels justified in following Mr Guzzard's footsteps as an organist instead of Sir Claude's as a financier, and goes to live with his predecessor Mr Eggleton who has also – and it seems definitively – lost a son in the war; while B. Kaghan and Lucasta who are not related by blood (a point the audience may by this stage be feeling some confusion about) can still as originally planned get married. The young people and Lady Elizabeth resolve to deal as best they can with the new realities; Sir Claude is left unreconciled: 'Do *you* really believe her?'

Even reduced to the briefest outline, there is still obviously quite a lot of plot here, when compared with Eliot's summary of *Murder in the Cathedral*. Nonetheless, as the first situation is deployed in the first act, and Mrs Guzzard's revelations come in the last act, there is something of a vacuum in act two, where one would expect to find the kernel within this highly decorated shell: the kernel is the feeling that the main characters, not merely Colby, have about their identity and destiny, but the identity question is also crammed into act one, and only repeated by Colby and Lucasta in act two, while the moment of communion between Sir Claude and his wife only develops in snatches as they prepare to meet Mrs Guzzard in act three.

In this hasty way, we find that just as Colby has always wanted to be a musician, so Sir Claude has always wanted to be a potter, both admitting they would not have been very good ones. Seen in terms of *The Cocktail Party*, finance and filial duty to which both have bowed lie on the lower, but still creditable path to spiritual truth, while art, which gives a mystic feeling 'an agonising ecstasy/Which makes life bearable' (CPP 466), is the higher path (though, confusingly, 'a kind of substitute for religion'). Colby then is meant to be making a higher choice as Celia does when he firmly rejects Sir Claude's claims, but this choice again shows a lack of humanity, even though Sir Claude's pain is acknowledged in the moment with which the play ends. Eliot had retrospectively considered Harry a prig; with Colby he seems to have created another, and one is left feeling that it is just bad luck for Sir Claude that he was not discovered to be the illegitimate son of a suburban potter during his formative years.

The positive side of this play appears in the number of satisfactory solutions to the problem of living in this world offered to its characters. Sir Claude and Colby agree in their experience of the world of absolute beauty, 'a world where the form is the reality,/Of which the substantial is only a shadow' (CPP 464), expressed by both in more Eliotian door-garden imagery: 'I believe you will go through your private door/Into the real world, as I do, sometimes' (CPP 465) and 'I turn the key and walk through the gate,/And there I am . . . alone, in my "garden"' (CPP 473), and though Colby fears that his garden is less real than Eggerson's real garden (Eggerson is a real gardener as he is a real Christian: neither are substitutes), at least this is better than stumbling around in a waste land like the characters in the earlier plays. The expression of these feelings, especially in moments of rare communication between characters, are the most forceful passages of the play. Otherwise the verse is, even more in this play than in the previous plays which have attracted the criticism, not really distinguishable from prose for most of the time. And there seems to be much more functional naturalistic prosaic language, because there is so much complex plot to be explained in a naturalistic style that requires interruptions, questions, digressions and repetitions.

The Elder Statesman (1958) is a coda to Eliot's work. His protagonist Lord Claverton approaches the question of identity from a new angle. Identity had not been Harry's pressing problem, and even less Becket's, but Edward and Celia and Colby and Lucasta had all voiced alarms about their sense of what they were really like and how this interacted with how others saw them. As in *The Confidential Clerk*, there is an emphasis on names. Lord Claverton began life as Dick Ferry, acquired his wife's name to become Richard Claverton-Ferry, MP as he rose in politics, and with the peerage dropped the Ferry altogether. Now retired for health reasons, entering a discreet convalescent home from which he may never return, he is forced to look back over his changing identity by the arrival of two figures from his past, ghosts in the Ibsenesque if not the supernatural sense. One is

Gomez, now a successful if shady businessman in South America, but once, under his real name Fred Culverwell, a fellow undergraduate, who was sent down from Oxford and then convicted of forgery, before Claverton helped him leave the country – he also recalls their night car ride in which a body on the road was driven over. Claverton is not criminally involved in any of this (though Eliot had intended at first he should be), but he had responsibilities for Gomez and for the body which he did not know to be already dead. Another guest is Mrs Carghill, who as Maisie Montjoy was expensively bought off when she threatened to sue him for breach of promise. She like Gomez, is nostalgic and very friendly – into which Claverton reads a threat if not of exposure then of constant recrimination. Claverton's third tempter is his own son Michael, who is another of his failures. It is he who brings the necessary change of heart to Claverton:

> What I want to escape from
> Is myself, is the past. But what a coward I am,
> To talk of escaping! And what a hypocrite!
> A few minutes ago I was pleading with Michael
> Not to try to escape from his own past failures:
> I said I knew from experience. (CPP 565)

He confesses his past to his daughter Monica, and in the telling does justice to 'my ghosts./They were people with good in them,/People who might have been very different' (CPP 571). In effect, his Furies have become kindly ones, though there is still a question mark over their joint efforts on behalf of Michael. His father, however, has to leave him to make his own salvation with a message of love instead of coercion, which may prove more effective. Eliot had said that he felt that *The Family Reunion* had needed completion by an *Oedipus at Colonus* and there are some similarities here in that the aged protagonists of both plays go away led by loving daughters and, after resisting messengers from the past, die reconciled with the gods.

The relationship to *The Family Reunion* is interesting, however, in that *The Elder Stateman* seems to be repeating rather than completing its predecessor. The chorus of Furies from the past is indeed integrated into the action, and the moment of transformation is more clearly marked as Claverton explains his change of heart and new relation to the past. The sense of doom haunting Harry is detached from its obscure relationship to a doubtful murder, and made explicit.

It's hard to make other people realise
The magnitude of things that appear to them petty;
It's harder to confess the sin that no one believes in
Than the crime that everyone can appreciate.
For the crime is in relation to the law
And the sin is in relation to the sinner.
What has made the difference in the last five minutes
Is not the heinousness of my misdeeds
But the fact of my confession. (CPP 573)

This is a suitable place to look back over the development of Eliot's plays. In pursuing the goal of a naturalistic representation of everyday life, at least the everyday life of a certain section of society, Eliot had to relinquish more and more his inclusion of the supernatural element, and with it the appropriateness and relevance of poetic expression. Some awkwardness and incongruity is erased, but the sense of everything on stage being in its way significant (as Harry's aunts and the cocktail party chat are significant of their own insignificance) is lost in the mundane necessity of getting from *a* to *b* in the plot. In the first three plays, Eliot had, if imperfectly, succeeded in much of his ambition, but whether one calls it going too far with naturalism or not far enough with poetry, from *The Confidential Clerk* his drama is less than poetic. As Martin Browne, who had to struggle with staging the poetic naturalistically, wrote to Eliot:

> I can't help feeling that the *Clerk* has taken you as far towards naturalism as you will want to go: and as I live with it I find that, with all its skill and fun and its impeccable choice of words, it does not grow on my affections as the others do. (EMB 294)

6
Poetic Drama in the Thirties

> Drama began as the act of a whole community. Ideally there would be no spectators. In practice every member of the audience should feel like an understudy.
>
> (W. H. Auden, *The English Auden*, p. 233)

Innovation and conservatism in verse drama in the 1930s meant that the field was far more heterogeneous and confused than before the movement started or than it is now that the tide has receded. Traditionalists like Gordon Bottomley were writing historical or folk plays, gradually introducing perhaps Yeatsian choral and dance elements; Yeats and Eliot themselves were still developing their personal styles; and new writers were beginning to appear in two distinct schools of dramatic production: the religious drama movement was promoting several verse plays by new and established dramatists; and borrowings from illegitimate drama, British and continental, from Russian ballet to cabaret, was inspiring secular experiments in little theatres in the metropolis.

This last tendency was both more distinct from other influences on poetic drama so far, and more innovative and prophetic of later dramatic development. It also attracted the most promising of the new generation of poets at least temporarily into the theatre. The plays, mostly produced under the aegis of Rupert Doone's Group Theatre, represented left-wing sympathies, and the poets were all from middle-class backgrounds: the most important dramatically were W. H. Auden and Christopher Isherwood.

Auden and Isherwood had met as young schoolboys at their preparatory school, and became friends at Oxford, and their collaboration of several plays followed from this. Basically, both had a strong dramatic tendency to externalise in their work. Isherwood's novels give an unusually large proportion of visualisable action and interaction between characters, while Auden, like Yeats, frequently assumed 'voices' or masks in his poetry. They could easily have become permanent participants in an accessible little theatre company, as Yeats had been, because Auden was involved in the new Group Theatre. They could, on the other hand, like Eliot, have persisted in seeking West End acceptance, but their dedication to the drama was never as strong as that of the elder dramatists, and they remained primarily poet and novelist.

Through another former school friend, Robert Medley, Auden had met Rupert Doone, the prime mover of the Group Theatre. Doone was a versatile man of working-class origins who had briefly danced as soloist in Diaghilev's company, then gained experience in the theatre, partly with Tyrone Guthrie at Cambridge. His unorthodox approach to theatre was based on his experiences in Paris, and meant that he was interested in integrating music, dance and mime with dialogue and plot. The Group acquired rooms where small productions could be put on, but took other theatres, such as the Westminster or the Mercury, when larger audiences were being sought. It was the verse dramas of poets like Auden and Spender that drew attention to the Group Theatre during the 1930s, and its work was known to a small, culturally aware segment of the theatregoing public, not to the public as a whole which Eliot was aiming at.

When in 1932 Auden stayed with Doone and Medley at their London flat, he agreed to write the outline for a ballet on the Orpheus theme, or a play based on the theme of the *danse macabre* – life as a dance of death. Abandoning the Orpheus idea after some labour on it, he finished *The Dance of Death* in 1933. Both Auden and Isherwood had enjoyed the cabarets of Berlin during holidays there, and Auden, like Eliot, approved of music hall: these influences made *The Dance of Death* less 'arty' and more 'popular' than its literary starting point might suggest. This was the period during which Auden was attracted by communism, and *The Dance of Death* begins with the announcement: 'We present to you this evening the decline of a class'. The central, non-speaking figure is the Dancer, who personifies capitalist values and seems also to have a will to self-destruction; he expresses both these elements in dance. There is an announcer who occasionally speaks for the Dancer, a 'theatre manager' who bustles in and out, and most of the other characters form a chorus, except for those who make scripted interruptions from among the audience. Roughly, the audience rebel against the Dancer's fascination, while the chorus are his eager dupes.

Perhaps because of the need to incorporate dance routines and songs, Auden constructed this play on more episodic, less plotted lines even than his later plays. For example, thc chorus is shown at first fawning on the Dancer, admiring his money, charm, beauty and leisure, until, unseen, he literally takes away the clothes from their backs; then stage hands bring on for them a basket of military uniforms, costumes from a patriotic musical, which prompts a reprise of martial song from the manager. The audience object to this:

> One, two, three, four
> The last war was a bosses' war.
> Five, six, seven, eight
> Rise and make a workers' state.

To which the chorus respond 'We will liquidate,/The capitalist state/Overthrow (DD 16). But then the Dancer dances a spell of persuasion that converts them from workers' revolution to a fascist 'reform', interpreted by the announcer: 'All this talk about class war won't get us anywhere. The circumstances here are quite different from Russia. . . . Our first duty is to keep the race pure, and not let these dirty foreigners come in and take our job' (DD 17). Other phases of the highly impressionable chorus's search for salvation include a 'back to Nature' move, and an attempt at transcendental mysticism, to 'fly alone/To the Alone' (DD 27). Twice the Dancer comes to grief, first by getting overexcited in the storms and shipwrecks following his fascist putsch, and finally by his ambitious flight into the mystic unknown.

Suitable to the title, the Dancer's death is accompanied by the transformation of stage and chorus into a decadent nightclub and its clientele, enacting their own *danse macabre* of 'amusements' and small talk. Though Auden brings in Karl Marx to deliver the *coup de grâce* with the curtain line 'The instruments of production have been too much for him./He is liquidated' (DD 38), his intervention is blunted by a lengthy 'will and testament' song on behalf of the Dancer, followed by an equally long hymn to hypocritical Britain by the chorus. This was to be the first of Auden's unsatisfactory conclusions, in that both he and Isherwood somehow could never shape their material to a suitable ending.

The Dance of Death was produced as a double bill with Eliot's *Sweeney Agonistes* in 1935, and here as in its first Sunday night performance in 1934, it attracted more enthusiasm for its theatricality than the enigmatic *Sweeney* did, enthusiasm more marked by comparison with the earlier poor reception of the published text. Most of the dialogue and chorus has little merit on the page, and its effect comes from juxtaposition with the bizarre and outrageous stage action. The perfunctory ideology does not redeem the text; it shows a heart in the right (i.e. left) place rather than a strong head. Auden's biographer Humphrey Carpenter quotes from an unpublished interview where he recalls:

> English Communism was insular. We knew what was happening in Russia. Purges and so on. But we felt England wasn't like that. We said 'Oh, you know how the Russians are, always violent. Here it will be different.'[1]

This is not quite the same as the Dancer/Announcer's proceeding to 'an English revolution' and from there to 'keep the race pure', but indicates vagueness about social change, and this is true of the collaborative plays too.

Another influence had already appeared in Auden's unperformed *Paid on Both Sides*, now included in collections of his longer poems. A strange dream sequence in the shape of a trial throws up classic Freudian symbols of psychological conflict and subconscious pressures, reinforcing the message that the hero's mother is responsible for forcing him to reopen the family feud. This is interpolated incongruously into the stark chronicle of the feud between Shaws and Nowers, whose terse and alliterative verse dialogue, quite unlike the banalities of *The Dance of Death*, comes from Auden's interest in Icelandic and Anglo-Saxon sagas. The Scandinavian laconic style did not reappear on the stage, unfortunately, but the Oedipal motif emerged again in the *Ascent of F6*.

Meanwhile Auden collaborated with Isherwood on *The Enemies of a Bishop*, a melodrama full of private jokes with poems by Auden interspersed, which was probably never suitable for public performance, and Auden alone wrote a play, *The Fronny*, now lost. After the comparative success of *The Dance of Death* Auden tried to reconstitute these last two dramatic pieces into a new play, *The Chase*, based on a comic quest for a missing aristocrat. Faber accepted it for publication, but Isherwood's comments on the manuscript evoked such wholesale reworking that it was transformed into the collaborative work eventually titled *The Dog Beneath the Skin* (1936). As in the draft, a villager, Alan Norman, is chosen by lot to set out on the quest for the missing Francis Crewe, accompanied by a mysterious stray dog. Isherwood not only cut out various subplots, but suggested the vital effect that the 'dog' is finally revealed as the missing Francis himself in dogskin disguise. The plot is episodic again, with Alan as an innocent abroad passing through benighted corrupt European civilisation: there is a court politely mourning for the dissidents who have been ceremonially shot; a night town of brothels and drug-sellers; a pleasure park; a hospital, and an asylum. The lunatic asylum is hardly more frenetic than any of the other scenes, even though some critics felt the satire of showing the lunatics responding to broadcasts of the country's dictator reduced real political threat to trivial farce. But as many plays from *Peer Gynt* to the *Marat/Sade* have shown, the behaviour of madmen, particularly en masse, easily becomes threatening and terrifying. Likewise the savage sequence in which Desperate Desmond slashes a Rembrandt as a cabaret turn, before the eyes of an appalled art critic and of the brutally laughing clientele, projects considerable violence. Another lighter scene is a conversation between Alan's left and right feet, which come out from behind a milestone to discuss their hard lot, and this is as much in the tradition of the early expressionists and surrealists as it is of music hall or pantomime. The episodes end with the return of Alan and Francis to the village, but Auden and Isherwood had difficulty in winding up the action. They tried various scenarios – in the text Alan and Francis defy the complacent village and leave; in the 1936 revival they tried having a village lady shoot Francis; and in 1947 she stabbed him, but none of these conclusions have much conviction. The effective verse given to the introductory chorus and to other characters during the play gave *The Dog Beneath the Skin* much more substance than *The Dance of Death*, and its theatrical inventiveness proved that the music hall or cabaret format could be an attractive vehicle – if there were any content to put into it.

The Ascent of F6 (1936) was intended to add psychological realism to the political message. Auden and Isherwood worked on the play in Portugal, and instead of a symbolic quest they built the play on a symbolic mountain climb. Auden knew several climbers, including his brother John, and saw that the theme offered as much conflict, suspense and scope for exploring character under stress as the war that was the subject of his next play. Again Auden and Isherwood divided the play between them. Isherwood wrote:

> Our respective work on this play was fairly sharply defined. We interfered very little with each other's work. The only scene on which we really collaborated was the last. It was understood, throughout, that Wystan's speciality was to be the 'woozy' and mine the 'straight' bits.[2]

The 'woozy' bits were the verse, but Auden also wrote some of the prose. The prologue begins with a page of elegant prose (and goes on for two more pages less elegantly) written by Auden and spoken by Ransom, the self-consciously named hero. He quotes Dante's account of Ulysses urging 'virtue and knowledge' on his men, questions the real motives of those 'seedy adventurers', these 'teachers without pupils, tormentors without victims, parasites without hosts, lunatic missionaries, orphans' (F6 14). He then questions Dante's own motives in turn:

> It was not Virtue those lips, which involuntary privation had made so bitter, could pray for; it was not Knowledge; it was Power. (F6 14)

This apparent digression lays out the main theme of the action. Ransom is required against his will to make a prestige dash to the top of the high unclimbed mountain F6 in a disputed foreign colony, before a rival imperial power can reach it. Ransom has always wanted to climb

F6, but simply because it was there, as it were, and not for dubious extraneous motives: he is definitely not interested in strengthening British claims to the colony, Sudoland. His refusal is overridden, as in *Paid on Both Sides*, by the emotional blackmail of his mother. An opportunity to withdraw is offered by the mysterious Abbot of a monastery on the glacier of F6; here Ransom sees in a crystal ball masses of mankind clamouring for him to save them: he could make this climb the path to celebrity and from there to beneficent power. This is Ransom's temptation by Power, as for Eliot's Becket, and the reminiscences of Eliot continue when the Abbot suggests he renounce the climb, to 'remain here and make the complete abnegation of the will' (F6 74). This would involve rites and rituals including dismemberment of corpses and of the 'esoteric body', recalling the fate of Celia in *The Cocktail Party*. The Abbot's words about the Demon which is supposed to haunt the mountain top are obviously Eliotian:

> He is – what shall I say? – the formless terror in the dream, the stooping shadow that withdraws itself as you wake in the half-dawn. You have heard his gnashing accusations in the high fever at a very great distance. You have felt his presence in the sinister contours of a valley or the sudden hostility of a copse or the choking apprehension that fills you unaccountably in the middle of the most intimate dinner-party. (F6 72)

But this is linked by Auden (one cannot doubt that this speech is a 'woozy' bit) to a psychological, not religious or metaphysical, explanation – the Abbot refers visions and demons to the repressed material of the subconscious.

The political component of the plot is underlined by the choral figures of Mr and Mrs A, who find distraction from their personal inadequacies and social dissatisfaction in the red herring of a 'climb story'. They speak in rhymed couplets of varied rhythms:

> MRS A: You see? The foreigner everywhere,
> Competing in trade, competing in sport,
> Competing in science and abstract thought:
> And we just sit down and let them take
> The prizes! There's more than a mountain at stake. (F6 82)

Much of this calculated banality is not as sharp as it might be; Auden did not seem to have a good ear for parodying clichés, and this weakens (Isherwood's?) naturalistic dialogue too where the chat of the four climbers bumps along in the rock-bottom style of the British B-movie, without either force of its own, or transformation into parodying comment on itself.

As usual there were problems with the ending. Ransom dies at the summit confronting the veiled 'Demon', symbol of all man's destructive tendencies, the fatal flaw that makes him vulnerable to the various temptations: the message is that external temptations are not the problem, it is the innate weakness that is to blame. A dream sequence as in *Paid on Both Sides* takes the form of a trial, and Ransom first accuses then tries to protect the Demon. In an Ibsenesque avalanche, the Demon is unveiled to reveal Ransom's mother. Ransom dies, in a mirror reversal of *Peer Gynt*, with his mother singing him an escapist lullaby, 'Reindeer are coming to drive you away' (F6 122). The culpability of the mother was emphasised in rewriting for the American edition, and a final scene of commentary was omitted in performance and later editions, but in a 1938 revival the mother unveiled only as a non-speaking figure.

Nonetheless the play was probably the most commercially successful of Auden and Isherwood's collaborations, filling the little Mercury theatre for two months, then running for five weeks in the West End. This encouraged the authors to a new effort, and Carpenter describes their decreasing sympathy with the Group Theatre:

> Auden went with Isherwood to a week-end conference at John Piper's country home to discuss the future of the Group Theatre. There, they behaved badly, failing to observe the timetable of events and generally fooling around, Auden strumming on the piano at all hours. They seemed to be impatient with the Group Theatre's aims now, and were certainly increasingly irritated by Ruper Doone. Robert Medley also had the impression that after the comparative commercial success of F6 they had tasted blood, and he gathered that they were planning for their next play something that would be a hit in the West End rather than cater specially for the Group Theatre's needs.[3]

As with Eliot, acceptability prompted a toning down of the poetry content, of which there is very little in the next play, *On the Frontier* (1938), and again as with later Eliot, the play was not a hit, nor did it run long anywhere. One problem is the confusing structure of the play: the European war between 'Westland' and 'Ostnia' is as much a prestige exercise as the climbing of F6, fuelled by a mad demogogue Leader and by Valerian, a cynical big businessman, and its appalling waste and suffering eventually provokes a workers' uprising. This is not really sufficiently prepared for, and the climax seems tangential to the body of the play. In production, the growing disaffection of the workers and soldiers suffers from being played during five interludes in front of the curtain (during scene changes), and though these are in verse and visually effective, the impact is reduced: the cramped parenthetic little scenes do not carry enough weight to counterbalance the warmongering capitalist establishment.

Alternating with the main scenes involving the political leaders, the lives of two ordinary families, one in each country, are shown as they become affected by the war. On stage this parallel development unfolds simultaneously; an invisible 'frontier' divides the stage down the middle so the audience can watch the families carry on their superimposed activities, conversations and quarrels, unaware of each other. The son and daughter of the respective families never meet, but are shown as somehow communicating in spirit, in

> the good place
> Where the air is not filled with screams of hatred
> Nor words of great and good men twisted. (OF 68)

This is both an ideal and an illusion, as the Eliotian imagery of the 'everlasting garden' and 'the threatening faces sudden at the window' suggests, and offers another contradictory message, implying that everything would be all right if people would just be good and let each other alone. Nonetheless the son, Eric, who starts the play as a pacifist, does not escape into dreams. We learn later that he has lost his pose as 'the sane and innocent student' and finds that neutrality assists injustice – unlike Lear, he cries 'None are innocent, none'. So he goes to the workers' barricades:

This struggle
Was my struggle. Even if I would
I could not stand apart. (OF 121)

But this is recounted in retrospect over his deathbed, and neither the uprising nor Eric's part in it is actually dramatised.

Auden and Isherwood did not and perhaps could not put on stage the problems of working people who were poorer than the office clerk level, and Stephen Spender suggested:

> The reason why the writers fail to present that 'other side' whose point of view they implicitly accept is because whereas they know a great deal about the side of the bourgeoisie – from which they consider themselves disinherited – they know far less about the workers' side which they believe themselves to have joined.[4]

On the other hand the song of the rootless, disaffected soldiers is vigorous, and reminiscent both of Brecht's songs in for instance *A Man's a Man* and of some of Auden's lyrics:

Ben was a four foot seven Wop
He worked all night in a bucket-shop
On cocoa, and sandwiches,
And bathed on Sunday evenings.

In winter when the woods were bare
He walked to work in his underwear
With his hat in his hand,
But his watch was broken.

He met his Chief in the Underground,
He bit him hard till he turned round
In the neck, and in the ear,
And the left-hand bottom corner. (OF 97)

On the Frontier was not produced at the Mercury theatre, though in the end Doone and Medley directed and designed as before, but in Cambridge, sponsored by Maynard Keynes, whose wife the dancer Lydia Lopokova played the daughter Anna. Benjamin Britten not only composed but played the score and Peter Pears acted in the chorus, but nonetheless the play was not liked, and its failure ended the hopes of commercial success.

Auden continued to write dramatically and semi-dramatically, for instance in libretti for operas, such as *The Bassarids* with Hans Werner Henze. His long poem *For the Time Being* was planned for Britten to set to music, and he translated *Don Giovanni* and *The Magic Flute*. In America Auden collaborated with the exiled Bertolt Brecht on a version of *The Duchess of Malfi*, an intriguing project which was cancelled by the arrival of the English director hired by the production company, Dadie Rylands, who insisted on producing the original Jacobean version. Auden had already seen at least *The Threepenny Opera* in pre-war Germany, though he claimed to be more influenced by cabaret, and he was initially sympathetic to Brecht, but Brecht's abrasive manner towards those who resisted his political or artistic dicta offended both Auden and Isherwood, so there were no more collaborations to lure Auden back into the theatre. Though he later translated some of Brecht's poety and songs into English, Auden carefully wiped the memory of their association from his mind.

Stephen Spender, a friend and fellow poet from their

Oxford days, wrote a poetic drama, *Trial of a Judge*, produced by Doone and the Group Theatre in 1938. This is a play which is difficult to read. It is full of strong situations, as it involves the murder of a Jewish intellectual communist, then later of his brother also, by a gang of fascists, together with the predicament of a judge who is pressed for political reasons to reverse the condemnation of the murderers. He does so, repents, too late, joins the communist protesters and eventually dies with them. But the impression is static: there are dream re-enactments of decisions taken, and everyone makes long and full statements of their positions, politely heard out by their interlocutors, rather than engaging in dialogue as such. Though the language is full of imagery it has an obscure and obscuring effect, and in spite of the four-stressed line, the verse is reminiscent of the more metaphysical kind of Elizabethan verse, partly due to the formal, slightly archaic style: for instance

For what is madness
Except a sense of final reality? (TJ 100)

The other friend and contemporary who attempted drama in verse was Louis MacNeice, whose stage drama *Out of the Picture* was produced, again by Doone and the Group Theatre, in 1937. Equally as comic and as indebted to music hall as the Auden–Isherwood plays, it also had rather more weight and complexity. Its hero, Portright, is an artist who despises money and success and prides himself on his Bohemian dedication to creativity as an end in itself. His narcissism provides much of the comedy, and his exaggerated indifference to everything else, especially the impending war, makes a satirical point. Much of the play is in prose, and there is a tendency to apologise for what poetry there is, in spite of its lack of realistic conventions. 'You speak very nicely' Moll says to Portright, and later '*I'll* talk a bit of poetry now' (OP 52). Though MacNeice was the son of a Northern Ireland clergyman who later became a bishop, he urges no religious solution (nor an atheist solution either) but seems to suggest liberal humanist commitment and action: 'taking action. Ever heard of action? It's something they do among the barbarians' says Moll witheringly. Moll is the model for Portright's one finished painting, and pities him at first, though she is hypnotised into being in love with him by the psychiatrist Dr Speilmann. The other main character is film star Clara de Groot, whom Speilmann, her analyst, shrewdly sees to be as 'cut off from the world of actual life' by her narcissism as Portright is, though he dare not tell her so. This farcical love plot (Portright also falls in love with Clara, perhaps as she is his female mirror image) is punctuated by interludes, some of which involve a radio announcer who, as in many modern comedy sketches, is shown performing all the programmes himself, with or without false moustaches, and so on. Apart from the necessary counterpoint of news of approaching war, these interludes add the weight and complexity mentioned above. For instance, a lecturer discusses Aristotle by negative reference to Chekhov, of whom Aristotle would have disapproved for mingling laughter and tears in the same art form – one is deep in a comedy and is suddenly faced with tragedy, the off-stage gunshot – this is inartistic. But it is also the method of *this* play: MacNeice piles on comic effects, such as a bailiff who intones in verse:

> Whoso walks in the ways of solvency
> He enjoys my respect and the absence of my person
> (OP 15)

but in the last act the impending war does break out, and the curtain goes down on the bombs and fires of an enemy air-raid. This incongruous mixture of comedy and tragedy works well because its theme is coherently but not crassly worked out, and has the same kind of fast-moving pace as the early Auden and Isherwood plays.

Much of the other poetic drama of the inter-war period was inspired by the revival of religious drama, in much the same way as Eliot's first works had been staged. Charles Williams was a friend of both Eliot and Auden, and is perhaps better known as a poet and novelist than a playwright. He was recognised by many as having a great personal sanctity. His editor, John Heath-Stubbs, recollects Williams telling him that he had been very much impressed by reading Yeats's *Countess Cathleen* as a young man, and suggests that Williams's style developed as Yeats's did, in parallel with his lyric poetry. His early plays are slight, but his *Thomas Cranmer of Canterbury* (1935) was commissioned for the Canterbury Festival and Martin Browne considered it a great play, as did Robert Speaight who played the title role, but later producers could never be persuaded to revive it. Williams's verse – which does not always use capital letters at the beginnings of lines – is similar to Eliot's Everyman style:

> Steed and speech go reined and spurred. I learned
> easier the riding than the reading; I took
> tenderness rather than tyranny and made my gain
> (CP 3–4)

though other passages in their continuous forward urgency and internal rhymes recall Hopkins:

When King Henry told me his dream I dared not speak
Of the beak of thc king's falcon, but well I knew
How it flew through my sleep, as now; a slither of
wings beats on my face and brings
a hot iron to my heart; (CP 45–6)

Thomas Cranmer, Henry VIII's archbishop, is a fascinating character but is expressed on the whole poetically rather than dramatically: Williams's interesting use of an ambiguous observer figure, the Skeleton, who comments on Cranmer's speeches, only prolongs his interior debate. As happens with many religious dramatists, the concentration brought by a well-defined subject was lost in diffuseness when Williams constructed his own plot for *The House of the Octopus* (1945), and the language becomes formal and stilted, most of the speakers in the play being non-English natives of a South Sea Island. The English missionary, Anthony, reverts to a Shakespearian or perhaps Victorian modified blank verse, and the result is a deadening effect on the play's Becketian, temptation-of-the-priest, theme.

E. Martin Browne had been active during the war in touring various religious plays, including *Murder*, with his own Pilgrim Players, often under difficult conditions, and after the war he put on a season of poetic drama at the Mercury theatre, including secular as well as religious plays. One of these, *This Way to the Tomb* (1945) by poet and playwright Ronald Duncan, was another work which somehow appealed to a wide audience where the author's other works did not. Some of its attraction lay in its unusual form, which separated the historico-religious area and the modern social-criticism area into two halves of the same play, called respectively Masque and Anti-masque. The first half tells of St Anthony's progress to sainthood, resisting external temptations, and also resisting the internal temptations represented by his three followers. Like Becket, Anthony has to learn that he must not even assert himself by seeking his own time of death, here by excessive fasting, but must await God's will with humility. The modern Anti-masque takes the form of a television programme trying to film the saint's fabled anniversary reappearance. Anthony appears as an Old Man, and is rejected by all except three of the onlookers, these three being identified with his three followers (played by the same actors, of course) illustrating the persistence of temptation and frailty as well as sanctity.

Some of the satire of the second half does in fact seem to bear out the 'Critic' in the audience who interrupts with

> One of the fundamental weaknesses of this play is, to my mind, the author's shallow conception of the people's fears. The novitiates we have seen are mere clay pigeons for the point of cheap satire, quite unrepresentative of the public's inarticulate spiritual dilemma. (TWT 82)

So far, those trying to move the saint by their complaints have been cardboard figures – the 'modern girl', or the 'aesthete' – their parts accompanied by 'blues' or 'boogie-woogie' music. But after the Critic's intervention the tone becomes more moving with the serious and lyrical appeal of two women, crying out against death and the meaninglessness of the human condition. The slightly sentimental ending is well prepared as Father Opine, the telly-sage of the programme, a typical sceptical guru, is finally brought to fulfil his role as the saint's third follower, with an appropriate renunciation of self-assertiveness and pride. Duncan chose a very difficult rhyming scheme which he manages without strain, but the confessional aspect of the play tends to give it an introspective, static effect. In spite of its popularity, some thought it more suited to the study than the stage, and Robert Speaight's memory of playing Anthony, for which he was placed on top of a rock and required to pour out his speeches from this vantage point, confirms the static effect in production.

There were several other writers of religious drama in verse at this time whose plays were not so widely known as Ronald Duncan's, since they wrote mainly for religious festivals in different parts of the country. These included Norman Nicholson, whose very North Country *The Old Man of the Mountains* (1945) opened Browne's season, Anne Ridler, who worked at Faber's, and Dorothy L. Sayers, best known as a classic detective story writer, and their plays tended to be seen by a special religious play audience as Eliot had predicted. It is also worth mentioning Gordon Bottomley, a dramatist of an older generation, who spanned both the Yeats and Eliot branches of writing. He began without really considering the current state of theatrical acceptability – he assumed that verse drama had always been written and always would be written. He was, like Yeats, interested in the Noh, and at various times adapted Yeats's chorus and symbolic costumes, and the folding and unfolding of a curtain-cloth, to his dramatisation of Celtic legends. He in fact developed a practice of choral movement as well as speaking, criticising the early Yeats for the immobility of his 'posing and speaking':

> the result was a visible monotony that bored the listener's eyes and gave his untrained ears more work

than they had been accustomed to, and he blamed the poetry.[5]

Much choral movement however, when not designed simply to point the verse – and evidently Bottomley's eye-catching chorus of seals, for instance, were trained to make seal movements rather than meaningful gestures – can give the eyes too much work, and a tendency to visual fussiness is evident in his adaptation of Yeats's clothfolding: his characters had to loop the long curtain with rings on and off a coat-hanger style 'holder', with endless possibilities for fiddling and distraction and things going wrong.

Bottomley was not ambitious to be a West End success, and so recalled that he had little difficulty in finding amateur companies to put on all his plays. Some of his work was produced by Terence Grey at his experimental Cambridge Festival Theatre company, one in a double bill with Yeats's *Fighting the Waves*. He also benefited from production in the poet John Masefield's private theatre built in his garden at Oxford, which had a 'double proscenium' or slightly smaller inner stage, which Bottomley believed to be particularly effective for poetic drama, and inspired him wishfully to design new theatres with apron stages and platforms, saying:

> Because I desire more speech and sound on my stage than the present all-pervading form of colloquial drama can give me: and as the theatres designed for that drama impoverish the delivery of my verse, I desire a different kind of theatre.[6]

But then under the auspices of the indefatigable Bishop of Chichester Bottomley took part in a discussion of religious drama with other poets, and was asked to write the *Acts of St. Peter* (1933) for the Octocentenary of Exeter Cathedral. His experience in seeing this play staged in Exeter Cathedral, St Margaret's, Westminster, and in Peterborough Cathedral changed his views on staging, and he declared 'formal drama can be performed here with an ease and acceptance never attained in a modern theatre building': he deduced that the ideal theatre space should be large, empty and adaptable, with a new stage built 'of estrades, rostrums and ramps'[7] for every play, an idea much like the aim of modern flexible studio theatres.

It seems then that verse drama at this time (and the trends of the 1930s went on into the 1940s after the war) was split into the two main areas of the episodic, blackly comic drama of the 1930s poets, and the formal, backward-looking religious drama. What the two areas had in common was the negative quality that they were not realistic. Realism is, one assumes, never to be eliminated in the theatre, but to include poetry in plays, a younger generation was to find that they needed to take the sort of eclectic approach that Auden and Isherwood had tried, and to attempt a mixture of styles as did Ronald Duncan, without his undramatic paralysis of the action while the poetry is going on.

7
Christopher Fry: Poetic Drama in Conventional Setting

Christopher Fry was born in 1907 in Bristol. He went to Bedford Modern School until he was eighteen, then took on a succession of theatrical or semi-theatrical jobs: he spent two brief periods teaching, but went back to the less secure but more congenial theatre work again. Among his longer lasting jobs was that of producer at Tunbridge Wells Repertory Company in 1934 to 1936 (at which point he married), from where he went to share the post of artistic director of the Oxford Repertory Company in 1939; he returned to this after the war. Thus his background is more in the theatre than any of his fellow dramatists. From adolescence Fry had written a series of plays, some of which were performed but not published. In a letter-preface to *A Sleep of Prisoners* Fry reminded Robert Gittings of how he

> persuaded me to take a holiday from my full-time failure to make a living, and sat me down, with a typewriter and a barrel of beer, in the empty rectory at

> Thorn St. Margaret. I had written almost nothing for five or six years, and I was to write almost nothing again for five years following, but the two months we spent at Thorn, to months (it seems to me now) of continuous blazing sunshine, increased in me the hope that one day the words could come. . . . The ten years in which you loyally thought of me as a writer when clearly I wasn't, your lectures to me on my self-defensive mockery of artists, and those two leisure months under the Quantocks, were things of friendship which kept me in a proper mind. (III 3)

This was the early 1930s, and Fry's playwriting was to begin, like Eliot's, with an amateur religious play, under the aegis of the movement for promoting religious drama sponsored by the Bishop of Chichester. This play, *The Boy with a Cart*, was performed in 1938, but Fry's next play, *The Firstborn*, was put aside during the war, completed in 1946, and not produced until 1948, after the first of what are remembered as Fry's characteristic poetic comedies, *A Phoenix Too Frequent*.

Fry's most productive period was in the 1940s and early 1950s when seven of his ten plays were first produced; after this, the new wave of kitchen sink drama, the enigmatic fantasies of the Absurdists, and Beckett's laconic plays moved interest and expectations away from the imaginative articulacy of Fry's characters. He said he 'went through a kind of crisis of confidence in my own ability to express the world as I saw it in terms of the modern theatre' (20C 186). Since *The Dark is Light Enough* (1954) he has written only the historical *Curtmantle* (1962) and the comedy *A Yard of Sun* (1970).

Because Fry was not an established lyric poet or indeed established as a writer of any kind before he wrote plays, as Yeats, Eliot, Auden and Isherwood were, his plays did not have their life prolonged by reflected interest in other works, after verse drama grew out of fashion. Again unlike Yeats or Eliot, Fry has not written at length about the form, content and philosophy of poetic drama and his plays in particular, but it is not true that, as Denis Donoghue claims, 'as a dramatist he has little to say'.[1] In the first place he reverses the approach of Yeats and Eliot by affirming that spiritual values, the call of the ideal or self-sacrifice, are equal in importance to material values, in the form of accepting and appreciating the multiplicity and beauty of the world. Earth is not a place of drudgery or a howling desert to Fry, far from it, but full of mystery, and 'wildly unprosaic'. Then, and sometimes in conflict with this, he tries to present man as partly a creature with an established relationship with the natural world, such as animals have, encoded in his genes or predestined by God, and also as having the yearning for a spiritual dimension within – not other than – the natural world. As he put it, 'the human being is struggling to achieve the end, or form, which already exists for him' (20C 187), an idea which he later recognised among the writings of Teilhard de Chardin. So by a circular route, his characters do often arrive at the point of having to reject mere gross materialism, but in the interest of fulfilling their earthly potential, and without supernatural sanction.

Fry supported his use of highly metaphorical verse by relating it to both the outward and inward qualities of the characters: 'Anyway I need to use verse when a speech has to become – how shall I say? – like an object reflecting that inner shaping of the character, that process of evolution' (20C 187). The inward qualities than are more important: 'It is an instrument which reflects the full life of man.' Fry is quite clear that he is not trying to pass off his verse as realistic everyday conversation: taking as his example a heroine waiting for her lover, he goes on:

> What, in common speech, she would say is something like 'Oh do, do, *do*, come back quickly, John!' It is not a very adequate demonstration of what her whole being is really saying. (20C 190)

In the earlier comedies the language was an assertive manifestation of the characters' thought and potential being and of the natural world in which they have to live. This gave rise to an image of Fry as an 'bacchic figure vomiting his careless words' as he ruefully protested, adding that the reality of the creative process was very different:

> having looked at this picture and marvelled, I turn back to my typewriter. Like an ancient Red Indian chief, I sit for some hours in silence. At last I am ready to speak, and say 'How', or perhaps some slightly longer word. My two fingers withdraw from the typewriter and the night wears dumbly on towards dawn.[2]

Fry's later plays have modified the exuberance of his style, and he did not claim to revere verbal fireworks above other elements in drama:

> The dramatist must view the world of his play, and the people of that world, with great precision: the poet-dramatist with the greatest poetic precision. The whole structure depends upon it, what scene follows another,

> what character goes and what character enters, where description or landscape becomes part of the action, or where it needs a bare exchange. The poetry and the construction are inseparate. Who understands the poetry understands the construction, who understands the construction understands the poetry, for the poetry is the action, and the action – even apart from the words – is the figure of the poetry.[3]

This is something like Cocteau's famous description of 'poetry of the theatre', the total dramatic effect, as opposed to 'poetry in the theatre', a recitation or reduction to decorative verbalisation: it is significant that Fry, whose elaborate style would seem to make him the typical 'poetry in the theatre' writer, insists so strongly that 'the poetry is the action'. Like Eliot, Fry also states that 'a verse play is not a prose play which happens to be written in verse. . . . It has its own nature'[4] but he aligns himself against Eliot with those who reject absolute realism; rhythm in verse has a powerful effect, which should not then be undermined by overlaying with the impression of casual speech rhythms but emphasised boldly: 'There is no need to do it by stealth'.

Practically, Fry did not set up rules for his work: probably his experience of a heterogeneous selection of theatrical productions left him with a pragmatic approach; audiences, he found, were happy both to relate to historical situations and to listen to contemporary figures speaking poetry, and misgivings on the subject were superfluous. Similarly, he said, 'I am never quite sure how much importance the kind of stage has in what I do – you write, on the whole, for what is there' (20C 188).

The Boy with a Cart (1938), though a minor piece, exemplifies Fry's subject matter and verbal style admirably, and like Eliot's early plays, shows dramatic techniques which the writer chose not to develop. Formally, it has elements in common with *Murder in the Cathedral*, including Chorus, mixture of prose and verse, and direct address to the audience. But in mood and tone it is quite the opposite of Eliot's play. It tells the story of young St Cuthman, who is inspired to take his widowed mother on a home-made cart to a distant village and build a church. Three miracles punctuate his adventures: jeering mowers are drenched in a localised downpour; obstructive villagers are compelled to pull the plough in the place of the oxen they have misappropriated; and, more seriously, the church's fallen king post is, off stage, replaced by Christ himself. So this saint, far from being the object of destruction, is constructive, is ultimately successful, and is beset with miracles instead of tempters. The chorus of the People of the South of England expresses experience as wholesome as those of the Women of Canterbury are disruptive:

> Sheepshearing, milking or mowing, on labour that's
> older
> Than knowledge, with God we work shoulder to
> shoulder; (I 7)

Their intimations of the supernatural are good and orderly, not evil and chaotic:

> Coming out from our doorways on October nights
> We have seen the sky unfreeze and a star drip
> Into the south: experienced alteration
> Beyond experience. We have felt the grip
> Of the hand on earth and sky in careful coupling. (I 8)

The grip of the hand is God's, reassuring. The syntax, structure and vocabulary – 'Not knowing yet, and yet sometimes discerning: / Discerning a little at Spring . . .', 'We have discerned a little, we have learned / More than the gossip that comes to us over our gates . . .', 'We have almost known, a little have known, / The work that is with our work' – are very close to that of Eliot's chorus. This is even clearer when Cuthman feels pain at the death of his father, and Eliot's characteristic repetition, and use of abstract nouns with definite articles are marshalled for an Eliotian purpose:

Out of this, out of the first incision
Of mortality on mortality, there comes
The genuflexion, and the partition of pain
Between man and God; there grows the mutual action,
The perspective to the vision. (I 16)

Apart from this style, Fry nonchalantly runs a whole gamut of speech patterns in this play. There is a subchorus of 'Neighbours' who comment on the plot as participants not narrators, in colloquial style but with occasional internal rhymes:

We have done what we could; we can't do more.
But he goes his own way, All that we say
He seems to ignore. He keeps himself apart,
Speaking only out of politeness
Eating out his heart. (I 17)

Cuthman and his mother speak their more serious material in verse and more mundane dialogue in prose; the unkind mowers have two songs with music, and Mother addresses the audience directly in prose, explaining how much time is supposed to have passed since the last episode. These changes of style are not meant to shock, or to make a point about theatricality, but to indicate a change of tone and suggest a change of attitude in the audience. It is the opposite of the smoothing over of transitions that Eliot came to aim at. *The Boy with a Cart* is a slight piece, and gave a prospectus of dramatic techniques, but Fry was not in fact to use many of them again: chorus, song and address to the audience were all discarded, and his other plays, though not imitating everyday modern life, each worked within its own theatrical illusion.

In Fry's other early religious plays, *The Firstborn* and *Thor with Angels*, both produced in 1948, the former at the Canterbury Festival, the latter at the Edinburgh Festival, there is more severity and less light-heartedness. *The Firstborn* is almost a tragedy, though its main character, the young Moses, triumphs over opposition, and the story tells of deserved punishment rather than tragic catastrophe: Pharaoh is repeatedly given the opportunity to let the Israelites leave, and is punished by plagues when he does not do so. The play ends, as the title suggests, with God's killing of the firstborn of all Egyptians, animals as well as human beings. The play deals with suffering and waste, from its opening, where Moses's arrival is a threat rather than a joy to the palace where he was brought up. The atmosphere is set by the screams of another Israelite dying at the task of building Pharaoh's tomb; then the plot moves from the Israelites' tents, where Miriam's embitterment counterpoints the desperate conspiracies of the few rebels, to the death of Pharoah's firstborn son, Rameses, a well-meaning innocent youth who had promised reform and liberalisation. The plot encompasses all the pain and loss and perversity that *The Boy with a Cart* had barely glanced at: Moses tells Anath his fostermother: 'Hell is old, but until now/It fed on other women, that is all' (I 118). The immunity of the successful Egyptians is an illusion, as perhaps one suspects of the fortunate People of the South of England.

Though a celebrator of the goodness of earthly existence, Fry gives full expression to the pessimistic view, and does not labour his response to it; the deaths of Rameses and the other sons 'link the ways of men and the ways of God with a deep and urgent question mark' (I 52) as he admits in the preface. Anath states it more specifically:

> What is this divinity
> Which with no more dexterity than a man
> Rips up good things to make a different kind
> Of good (I 119)

and Moses states his three possible reactions to this destruction: to give way under his guilt for the divine destruction; to adopt a black view of all human destiny, proceeding 'by guilt and guilt'; or to see Rameses as taken into immortal life, forever 'here, pursuing the ends of the world' (I 140). Fry realised afterwards that the significance of Rameses, and of Moses's final recovery from his 'momentary spiritual death' had escaped his audiences, and said 'I have been learning too reluctantly that neither audiences nor critics are clairvoyant'; even with a play by no means as metaphysical as Eliot's, verse made more difficult, not clearer, the expression of complex concepts if they were not given due space for expansion.

The verse here is rhythmically uniform; all dialogue is

in the sophisticated, articulate style of Cuthman's verse dialogue; the vocabulary is forceful and full of imagery. Denis Donoghue objects that everyone speaks the same imagery, and that Miriam's 'I repeat myself unendurably like the Creation' is not her but Fry's tone:[5] however this wry irony is characteristic both of her and of Anath, two experienced and embittered women, while the Pharaoh and his son use more sober pictures, such as 'the future's loping footfall', or time with 'bony spade' heaping up age; and Moses's brother and nephew, less imaginative, use very few images at all.

Thor with Angels is written in a similarly articulate and imagistic language, with the addition of occasional alliteration, as suitable to this story of Jutes conquering Saxons and being required to receive the gospel of the Christian God from Augustine. Though Merlin curiously appears, unearthed from hibernation to fulfil a kind of choric role, he remains within the action, if prophesying beyond it. Again there is a difference not only in vocabulary but in rhythm between the abrupt, short sentences of the Jutes, and Merlin's rambling verse paragraphs which, perhaps because of the magician's Celtic origins, have a ring of Dylan Thomas:

> the end of the throes of sleep
> Where the stream of the dream wakes in the open eyes
> Of the sea of the love of the morning of the God.
>
> (II 102)

Fry here is trying to unite Christian belief and the right to life and joy in the created world of nature, in opposition to the Norse gods, life on sufferance, and the fearful sense of being 'the eternal alien in our own world'. Death hovers somewhere in most of Fry's plays, throwing into relief the vigorous life he is placing before us. He suggested 'If we don't love life and value it deeply our acceptance of death becomes meaningless, a shrug of the shoulders instead of an ultimate act of life'.[6] Only the deluded Dynamene and Thomas, and the perfect Countess Rosmarin accept death; others like Hoel, the young Briton killed by pagan captors in *Thor*, protest loudly and unheroically 'I want to live' (II 73).

Certainly *A Phoenix Too Frequent* (1946) is an argument against despising the world. It is set in a tomb, but the tone of the dialogue referring both to the newly dead Virilius and to the prospective suicide of his young widow Dynamene is light, even frivolous, and assures us that there is no real cause for concern. The proposed death by self-starvation of Dynamene and her maid Doto is both insufficiently motivated, for their grief is qualified by poetical digressions, and inadequately planned, for both ladies complain and are seriously discouraged by trivia like cold hands and no breakfast. When Dynamene laments

> Oh poor Virilius! To be a coming man
> Already gone – it must be distraction. (II 9)

the language is not degrading a profound grief, but showing up its superficiality. The way Dynamene speaks, for instance in a speech characteristic of Fry's early comedies:

> What a mad blacksmith creation is
> Who blows his furnaces until the stars fly upward
> And iron Time is hot and politicians glow
> And bulbs and roots sizzle into hyacinth
> And orchis, and the sand puts out the lion,

Roaring yellow, and oceans bud with porpoises,
Blenny, tunny and the almost unexisting
Blindfish; throats are cut, the masterpiece
Looms out of labour; nations and rebellions
Are spat out to hand on the wind – and all is gone
In one Virilius, wearing his office tunic. (II 12)

contradicts *what* she is saying – she is still very aware of all these fascinations of nature, and the loss of Virilius has not made her forget them. Tegeus, a soldier guarding the bodies of six executed men outside the tomb, is the spokesman for continuing life. He is at first overcome with admiration to find the tomb inhabited by such a dedicated self-sacrificing woman. It is he who makes the remark 'Death is a kind of love' which Fry later explained as having at least 'one very human meaning',[7] that is, to acquiesce in becoming one with the earth in the cycle of life and death. Tegeus finds this absolute sacrifice encouraging: 'To have found life after all unambiguous!' (II 18). The illusion of simplicity does not last very long, as Tegeus falls in love with Dynamene and finds himself persuading her *not* to be faithful and self-sacrificing. Aided by a large bottle of wine, he succeeds, and then a comic reversal brings him, when he discovers that one of his corpses has been stolen in his absence, to choose suicide as a quicker and nobler way of forestalling execution for dereliction of duty. The reversal is complete when Dynamene has the inspiration of substituting Virilius's corpse for the one that was stolen. The audience here may well agree with Tegeus's protests that 'It's terrible, horrible' (II 48) – has comic questioning gone too far, and ended by belittling Tegeus's pro-life arguments, in that such a total alteration in Dyamene suggests that she found it quite easy to change her mind?

Fry's comic début here was due to the influence of E. Martin Browne, who asked him to write the play for the same season of poetic plays at the Mercury which had begun with Nicholson's *The Old Man of the Mountains* and Duncan's *This Way to the Tomb*. The *Phoenix* was extremely popular, and was revived at the Arts theatre later in the year with Paul Schofield as Tegeus, and this led directly to Fry's writing *The Lady's Not for Burning* for John Geilgud, *Venus Observed* for Laurence Olivier, and *The Dark is Light Enough* for Edith Evans. Browne suggested that Fry's meteoric rise was partly due to his counteracting post-war austerity – there was a need for richness and frivolity and extravagance, as a sort of equivalent to the New Look in fashion, perhaps. The fact that Fry's style was sustained over four comedies earned him his reputation as a leader of the poetic drama movement along with Eliot, while other dramatists had achieved one successful play then dropped from view.

In the full length *The Lady's Not for Burning* (1948) Fry reworks the theme of *A Phoenix Too Frequent*. It contains another character, Thomas Mendip, who clamours for death because he is tired of life. He is one of four young men in the play, the others being the mayor's two nephews, Humphrey and Nicholas, competitive and volatile youths, and his nice young clerk, Richard. Only two young women appear, one being Alizon, brought out of her convent to be betrothed to Humphrey, and Jennet Jourdemayne, the 'Lady' of the title, who is hunted, arrested and threatened with burning for being a witch. So the play soon offers two possibilities of death, one whimsical, one serious, and in spite of the comedy of the mayor's unruly household, Jennet's desperate wish not to die casts a darker shade than Thomas's theatrical embitterment. Of course Jennet and

Thomas fall in love, though he resists the temptation to take an interest in life for as long as he can. The plot is neatly resolved on one level by the fact that Thomas's claim to hanging and Jennet's condemnation to burning rest on their having respectively murdered and transformed into a dog the rag and bones man, Old Skipps. When Old Skipps turns up at the end, alive, well and drunk, both cases for punishment are seriously undermined.

The shadow over the play is not a very dark one however, and productions tend to dispel it. According to E. Martin Browne's wife, Henzie Raeburn, who played the mayor's sister in the first Arts theatre production, the director Jack Hawkins mistrusted the dramatic effect of Fry's poetry and filled the play with frenzied movement and business to pre-empt possible boredom, and when the play was nonetheless so successful that it was revived the following year at the Globe theatre, with John Geilgud directing and playing Thomas Mendip, and Richard Burton as Richard, Claire Bloom as Alizon, and Pamela Brown as Jennet, the effect was still more cheerful and light-hearted than Fry had intended. Thomas is an ex-soldier who has been fighting in Flanders, and Fry later said that he had had in mind the war-shocked, embittered, disaffected men who could be seen tramping the countryside after any major war. Geilgud's bright, debonair Thomas had not, however, conveyed this. Fry thought that a subsequent production where Thomas wore a big ragged garment suggesting a First World War army greatcoat and behaved with more savagery was nearer to his conception, but he admitted that his own writing was not guiltless here: Thomas claims death in such whimsical circumlocutions that it is hard for the audience to take him any more seriously than the mayor does. Similarly, the scene where Thomas and Jennet enter, having been put to the thumbscrew, gives very little verbal impression that they have undergone real torture. To reach Fry's own unfulfilled purpose, it is necessary for a director to work *against* the author's text, which in a production aiming to appeal to post-war optimism would seem a perverse thing to do.

The mechanism of the plot is not the only moving force for the characters, however. Greed, superstition and bloodthirstiness of mob and mayor have insisted on Jennet's guilt virtually regardless of the Old Skipps pretext, and it is the reassertion of human kindliness that really saves her. The mayor weeps, trying to assert her guilt, and Justice Tappercoom finally hints that as nobody is watching she should simply make her escape. Thomas allows Jennet's attractions to reconcile him to life, and all ends well. The humanity is not asserted too easily: Jennet is made to consider the reduction of her will to live to the ignoble plea for life at any price. Humphrey offers to save her if she will sleep with him. She considers this without prejudice, but feels that everything would be cheapened and spoilt if she accepts the bargain. But she hesitates, balancing her sense of her own integrity with her need to live, and this serves to redeem the love of life in the play from the accusation of gross materialism.

The play had been planned as

> one of a series of four comedies, a comedy for each of the seasons for the year, four comedies of mood. I don't know whether a comedy of mood is an accepted category, or whether it's something I've coined to cover my particular aim. It means that the scene, the season and the characters, are bound together in one climate.[8]

This is the spring comedy, set in spring and incorporating an April-like alternation of laughter and tears; it also is laden with imagery, from Thomas's early remark:

> you're desperate
> To fly into any noose of the sun that should dangle
> Down from the sky. Life, forbye, is the way
> We fatten for the Michaelmas of our own particular
> Gallows. What a wonderful thing is metaphor.
> (II 119)

to Jennet's caution as they finally make their escape:

> That was the pickaxe voice of a cock, beginning
> To break up the night. (II 212)

Apart from the decorative and comic effect – everyone speaks in images which amuse by their originality, just as everyone in prose comedies consciously or unconsciously 'makes jokes' – the imagery evokes and insists on the beauty and presence of the natural world, from blisters to cuckoos to caddis flies to the moon and stars. It is the predestined, purposeful work of God, as Thomas explains, inevitably laid down in its own being:

> I can pass to you
> Generations of roses in this wrinkled berry.
> There: now you hold in your hand a race
> Of summer gardens, it lies under centuries
> Of petals. What is not, you have in your palm.
> (II 171)

Within this world we find man, part natural, part striving for something more than mere nature:

> driven and scorched
> By boomerang rages and lunacies which never
> Touch the accommodating artichoke
> Or the seraphic strawberry beaming in its bed.
> (II 173)

Fry's next comedy laid out the same view of man and nature, in hardly less extravagant language, in *Venus Observed* (1950). This play is set in the present. Although Fry disagreed with Eliot's view that historical costume and setting were too easy, a way of making poetry acceptable, nonetheless all his plays so far had been set in the past, severally in biblical, classical, dark and mediaeval ages. Now, bypassing the Renaissance altogether, he produced in 1950 and 1951 two plays with modern settings, one each in his favourite genres of seasonal comedy and religious drama. *Venus Observed*, written for Lawrence Olivier who played the Duke of Altair in it, is the autumnal comedy of the set: 'the season is autumn, the scene is a house beginning to fall into decay, the characters, most of them, are in middle life', Fry wrote. Within this framework the theme is loneliness and incompleteness of human life, 'a space of the heart, or the mind, unsatisfied'. It is worked out mainly through the central plot of the Duke's search for completion in love, in a way that has eluded him in all the temporary love affairs he has had since his early widowhood. He asks his grown-up son Edgar to choose for him between three former mistresses, Rosabel, Jessie and Hilda, signifying his choice by the classic award of an apple. Apart from these main characters, there are some comic servants and an estate manager, Reedbeck, whose daughter Perpetua arrives back from America just in time to dazzle the Duke into second thoughts about his marriage plan.

Perpetua represents perpetual youth as well as perpetual beauty and is more suited for the younger generation than for an autumnal duke – such is Edgar's indignant reaction when required to give her the ducal apple:

> I will offer her
> The cloudy peach, the bristling pineapple,
> The dropsical pear, the sportive orange,
> Apricot, sloe, King William, or a carillon
> Of grapes, but not, as God's my judge, an apple.
> (I 177)

As well as the interrupted choice, there are two other situational set pieces, neither necessarily autumnal, but both implying change and destruction. The first is an eclipse of the sun, which is the pretext for gathering the lady candidates in the Duke's observatory: Fry thought it implied 'the eclipse of the "animal passion" in a man' and 'the eclipse of life itself in the shadow of death'.[9] The Duke is refusing to be eclipsed, by pursuing the youthful Perpetua, and his passion is perhaps symbolised in the second crisis, when he and Perpetua are trapped in a fire which burns down his east wing, observatory and all.

Fire rather than eclipse has been the dominant image in production. Olivier, like later directors, tended to highlight the witty interaction of the dynamic Duke and his eternal polygon of satellite ladies. Like Thomas Mendip, the Duke is articulate in excess of what is necessary – his son pointedly has to bring him back to 'What we were talking about when you started talking' – and this fecundity gives the impression in performance of growth rather than decay. Fry had envisaged the play as embodying a strange, crumbling world, pervaded by the knowledge of death, but again admitted that both production and writing had wandered away from this.

Perpetua's terror-stricken declaration of love to the Duke as the flames rise around them is an ineffectual but understandable by-product of fear, a grasping after life. Neither the lady nor the gentleman are for burning in the play; they are rescued, and Perpetua firmly recants her false declaration. The fire itself is a powerful dramatic element; it not only reflects the Duke's self-will and passion, but the effect on man of suffering and mortality generally. The fire was started not by accident, but by Rosabel, the most sensitive of the Duke's past mistresses, who wants to teach him not to be so indifferent to his effect on others. She planned for him to lose his observatory, symbol of his lofty surveillance of the universe, but in fact he is more affected by the denial of his fire-inspired hope of winning Perpetua. Perpetua too learns from this that her youthful insistence on independence is not so easy:

> I'm still remembering
> I can give pain, and that in itself is loss
> Of liberty . . .
> No one is separate from another; how difficult
> That is. I move, and the movement goes from life
> To life all round me. And yet I have to be
> Myself. And what is my freedom becomes
> Another person's compulsion. (I 244)

The Duke, learning the same thing late in life, only after this disappointment realises 'Rosabel is hurt'. He decides to marry Rosabel (after she has expiated her arson in the local gaol) and has two Keatsian arias to express his reconciliation to the joys of maturity:

> The landscape's all in tune, in a falling cadence
> All decaying. (I 245)

and with irrepressible enthusiasm, he is soon congratulating himself on the prospect of

> Shootings, stabbings, lynchings of the limbs,
> A sudden illumination of lumbago.
> What a rich world of sensation to achieve. (I 247)

The language of the play is as full of verbal wit and surprising images as its predecessors, reflecting the exuberant character of the Duke, but all the characters are highly aware of their surroundings and ready to discuss the interaction of world and man. Even as apparently superfluous an excursus as Edgar's description of his horses, Fry noted, was intended to stress the natural wonder of the living creature as part of what he sees as the pattern of things. The Duke explains the theme of the play, the loneliness of man, his 'Estrangement in a world/Where everything else conforms' and where all other life has its complete destiny imprinted in it, like Thomas's rosehip. Until love, or some other form of dedication gives man 'a complete, unsolitary life' (I 201) the natural world is a reminder of what he has not. In the end of the Duke learns to sink self-assertion in acceptance and thought for others: this scene, Fry thought, was played 'absolutely magnificently' by Olivier, uniting the idea of rebirth and acceptance of death with a hopeful, melancholy, rueful tone that gave the final cadence to the play.

The Dark is Light Enough (1954) is the 'winter comedy' and does not involve the comparison with the natural world in its exploration of how much one should value life, a theme now brought to the forefront of the plot. The protagonists here are the Countess Rosmarin and the very dislikeable Richard Gettner, a kind of angry young literary figure, once married to the Countess's daughter, and the play opens amid the Hungarian uprising against the Austrian occupiers in 1848, with the Countess rescuing Gettner who has joined, then deserted, the Hungarian patriot army. She is the kind of virtuous, witty, kind, endearing character that is as much a gift for an actress as the Duke of Altair is for an actor; Edith Evans was convincingly magnetic without whimsy in this part, though a number of critics referred to her previous triumph as Millamant in Congreve's Restoration comedy, *The Way of the World*, which confirms the rather exhibitionist effect of the production. Oliver Messel's elaborate set, critic Caryl Brahms noted, was so full of visual nooks and crannies as to distract from the action: a Fry play had become an opportunity for display.

Gettner, on the other hand, is determined to be despicable: his life has no sentimental appeal, it is simply a life:

> I'll not die to oblige anybody;
> Nor for the sake of keeping up
> Decent appearances. Before I do
> I'll get down on all fours, foot-kissing,
> Dust-licking, belly-crawling,
> Any worm can have me for an equal,
> Rather than I should have no life at all. (III 86)

The Countess is in the winter of her life for, though not very old, she is very ill, and she dies leaving Gettner the trust of meeting and deflecting the Austrians in pursuit of his own former pursuer. It is without any illusions of heroism or love that he waits, as the curtain falls, to prove he has some values above the merely animal by confronting the Austrians.

Gettner is in the winter of his talent as a writer, as well as in his other fortunes: he feels inadequate:

> Reality itself, with wonder and power,
> Calls for the sound of great spirits
> And mocks us with a wretched human capacity.
> (III 109)

So although he at least among the cast is potentially a poet, his chastened language matches that of the rest of the characters. Words are used with weight and attention to secondary meanings and associations but there is little image-making or prolonged word-spinning in the manner of the previous two comedies, and less working of words for all they are worth than in *The Firstborn*. One effect of more weight and less flow in the style seems to be that the actual lines and line endings of the verse have more relation to sense and importance of meaning than in the earlier plays, where the divisions sometimes appear quite arbitrary. Here not only do the line endings occur in more natural junctures, but they are used in positive rhythm. Gettner's patriotism was inspired – suitably to his role as angry young man – as a challenge to the overbearing Sunday church bells:

> Bash, crash, take that for your damned impudent
> Soul, they said; in the name of the Father, the Son
> And the Holy Ghost, bash, bash: we'll lay you
> Flat in the mud of Crown Prince Rudolph Street,
> You dust. (III 79)

The irregular rhythm and the unexpected pauses here reflect the uneven rushes and hesitations of hand-pulled bells, concentrating on sound.

Looking back to Fry's other modern play, *A Sleep of Prisoners* (1951), verbal dexterity is carried as far as Fry ever extended it, before his move towards simplicity. The sleep of the four prisoners-of-war, locked in some foreign church, consists of a series of waking dreams, in which they re-enact certain biblical episodes; from the initial ordinary chat before they settle down to sleep, deliberately unenterprising – 'How can I help it if I can't work myself up/About the way things go? It's a mystery to me' (III 10) – the dream language follows Freudian interest in association, jokes and misuse, though the depths the dreamers plumb are philosophical rather than sexual. For example, Peter's summary of Nebuchadnezzar's speech effectively parodies the menacing platitudes of every power leader in its nonsense:

> What bastard language
> Is he talking? Are we supposed to guess?
> Police on earth. Aggression is the better
> Part of Allah. Liberating very high
> The dying and the dead. Freedoom, freedoom. (III 49)

In the preface Fry mentioned his preoccupation with 'what makes for life and what makes for death' and his previous attempts to 'find a way for comedy to say something of this, since comedy is an essential part of men's understanding', this play being 'a more simple statement' (III 3). In the Cain and Abel episode, his earlier conflict between the complete, purposeful natural world and incomplete, questing mankind causes the hostility between Dave-Cain, 'Amply the animal is Cain, thank God', and Peter-Abel, 'Expecting purpose to keep her date' (III 19). The only solution to man's unfulfilled state is daring to follow the Good. Meadow's speech in the fiery furnace could apply to Countess Rosmarin:

> Good has no fear
> Good is itself, whatever comes,
> It grows, and makes, and bravely
> Persuades, beyond all tilt of wrong. (III 54)

The Cain–Abel motif gives a clue to the theme of *Curtmantle* (1962) which otherwise is a chronological portrait of Henry II, Curtmantle being his nickname. His conflict with Thomas à Becket dominates the first half of the play, and overshadows the rest of his life. Henry's object in life is to restore law and security to his kingdom, after the chaos of civil war, and Becket's different priorities threaten this object. In their encounters, then, Henry upholds the practicalities and material satisfactions of man's life, while Becket stands for its mysteries. Becket asks 'Whether indeed there can ever be a world/Answering to the man created?' but Henry sees this satisfactory world as not only possible but achievable by himself. It might seem that in making Henry so evidently unimaginative in his imaginative programme, Fry must be condemning him, for Henry keeps insisting on simplicity: 'truth is unalterable, the truth being one' (III 199); 'One order is going to be saved: mine in this kingdom!' (III 220); 'the house is a single thing' (III 232); and 'the voice of Plantagenet is one voice' (III 233). Against him are the voices of Becket, 'The truth, like all of us, being of many dimensions' (III 199), of Eleanor his wife, 'this hidden law may prove to be/Not your single world, not unity but diversity' (III 259), and of his sons

'Each of us against the other' (III 261). But Becket is unreliable and destructive too. His fluctuations about whether or not to submit to the king, agreeing then rescinding his agreement when it is to be put in writing, are as confused as Henry's assumptions, and Fry's initial concept was sympathetic to Henry's audacious vision: 'I couldn't understand why it was Becket, and not Henry, who had had the plays written about him. I came to understand later!' (20C 186).

The alternative to these 'two men in a rage' is Eleanor's suggestion, both more practical and more mystical, of compromise and experiment:

> Consider complexity, delight in difference.
> Fear for God's sake, your exact words.
> Do you think you can draw lines on the living water?
> Together we might make a world of progress.
> Between us, by our three variants of human nature,
> You and Becket and me, we could be
> The complete reaching forward. Neither of you
> Will dare to understand it. Have I spoken too late?
>
> (III 225)

This has some relevance to the structure of this ambitious play itself. It begins with the chaos of a temporary night encampment of the king's travelling law court, and it ends in a similar chaos of retreat from Le Mans, Henry's birthplace, which he has accidently set on fire. However, the vigour and diversity of these scenes is diluted in the central chronicle of Henry's life. There are some powerful episodes, such as the confrontation of Henry, Becket and the bishops in a fog-yellowed, surrealistic winter morning, or Henry's response to the news of Becket's murder, his Lear-like rage appropriate to the situation:

> No men are fit live, no-one in the world!
> Foul and corrupt, foul and corrupt. All
> Contagious. All due for death. Why should I spare
> A man who can bear life and bring its messages?
> (III 252)

falling to a pathetic hope that the message was an illusion 'only here in my head'. But the continuous flow of the action, time passing in a momentary black-out or the Marshal's narrative interruption, levels down the significance of events, and the stating and restating of positions, narrative and retrospective, encumber the moments of vivid life. The situation of writing 'a strictly historical play' was not in tune with Fry's poetic style; everyone speaks a little portentously, because their words are going to be historically important, and none permit themselves the daring of the later mediaeval *Not for Burning* characters.

It seemed that with this play, seven years after his previous one, Fry was either finishing his career with aplomb or taking an entirely new direction, but in fact after about an equal interval he wrote in 1970 *A Yard of Sun*, subtitled a summer comedy, completing his seasonal set and ousting the claims of *A Phoenix Too Frequent* to that title. This play gathers a highly vocal, mainly related group of people in one place – the forecourt of a town villa – as all the comedies do; but here the setting is Italy just after the Second World War. Angelino the caretaker has two sons (and a third absent whom he never mentions) who quarrel as vigorously as the young Plantagenets, Roberto being a revolutionary doctor (a rifle in one hand, a stethoscope in the other), and Luigi a former fascist collaborator and would-be politician, easygoing but corrupt. This dialectic is extended when the third son of Edmondo appears, having made good shadily as a business man, and now rich enough to hire the palazzo his father looks after. The mood, setting and characters are part of a summer of a Mediterranean kind, with great heat, frayed tempers, thunderstorms and folk festivities, rather than the decorous flowery English summer. The language similarly is not flowery, but frequently colourful in its inventiveness: Cesare, the neighbour returning at last from a German prison camp, suffered an unhappy marriage when he felt 'The sky draw away from him' and even now, settled with the kind Giosetta, 'Questions would come rolling over him/Like tanks every now and then'. The innovativeness is not completely taken for granted – Giosetta half apologises for Angelino's eloquent consolation by saying 'Trust you to make an opera out of it'. In fact the plot centres on the 'Palio', a pageant-cum-horse-race which is said to 'surpass in appeal and impact, the most splendid shadows of Verona's operas' (YS 113). This off-stage festival is not a mere revival: for the participants, acquiring their involvement at birth, 'are, not act, what we see' (YS 112). Spectators and protagonists are united in more than mere enjoyment: 'To participate to belong, to be'. The experience of unity is exemplified also in the characters of the play. In spite of apparent conflicts, they do not need Edmondo as a *deus ex machina* to alter their lives. Roberto of course rejects capitalist interference; Luigi is happy to be helped but independently manages to acquire fame, influence and admiration in the city by riding (and falling off) the winning horse in the Palio; and even Angelino, offered his dream restaurant to manage, finds he does not want it. Luigi's self-seeking is as skin deep as Roberto's Henry-like faith in political systems: in practice he treats his patients with humanity not exhortation:

'You made them laugh./You somehow changed each room/Into a little ark bobbing on the flood' (YS 61). As Cesare explains, the lesson to take away from the prison camp is of man's humanity, not his inhumanity, to man: 'Insist on all the powers that recover us' (YS 104).

Fry's charitable view of mankind puts him at odds with his contemporaries, and the positive assertiveness of his language provokes critics to regard his work as like plum cake, too rich and too sweet. In reading, the melancholy undertow is evident, but it seems to be lost under the additional layers of an actor's charm in production. Kenneth Tynan called Fry 'a producer's nightmare', while praising his verse as 'not cryptic and solemn, needing sombre pointing and emphasis, but trickling, skimming, darting like a salmon in a mountain stream';[10] Geilgud's production of *The Lady's Not for Burning* had tamed this into a 'beige conversation piece'. His work has been compared with Restoration comedy, which may also have implications about production style. When Fry was writing, productions of Restoration comedy were of the pretty and mannered variety. Later, in the 1960s and 1970s, directors stressed Restoration savagery and pessimism beneath the comic surface. Fry is not pessimistic, but perhaps needs a little sombre pointing and emphasis to stress what his style is stylish *about*.

8
New Directions in Poetic Drama: the Position Today

I am pleading for the revival of poetic drama, no less!
(John Arden, *New Theatre Magazine*)

From being an important force in British drama – the major movement since Shaw or the Manchester School – poetic drama wavered into the 1940s and 1950s, then seemed to go into eclipse as the New Wave of Osborne, Wesker, Arden and Pinter broke over it in the mid 1950s. Critics of this new wave said that it was merely an updated version of the old naturalism, extending the permissible boundaries further than before: certainly it seemed to be undoing everything Eliot had tentatively attempted.

At about the same time, Absurd drama introduced an influence quite opposite to realism – unrealism, one could call it. By the end of the 1960s the cross-fertilisation of these schools meant that a widespread and popularly accepted sort of play was a mixture of realistic, especially socially critical elements with openly theatrical and non-illusionist elements. The Auden and Isherwood plays were the nearest precursors to these in England, but there is almost certainly no direct line of influence, merely an indication that the earlier dramatists were ahead of their time.

Although religious drama continued to be written for various churches and festivals into the 1940s, no other secular verse dramatist really challenged Fry and the ageing Eliot. Louis MacNeice, whose *Out of the Picture* had been promising, went to work for the BBC and either because of this or because there was no post-war theatre or audience he cared for, wrote thereafter solely for the radio. His *Christopher Columbus* (1944) told the story of the explorer in verse with solo voices to represent abstract qualities, and in the preface he made some observations about the genre: radio drama must move on a fairly primitive plane to keep the listening attention of a wide audience, comparable in some ways to that of the bards of the oral tradition. *The Dark Tower* (1946) seems to have been the play he felt was most successful: both in its quest form and some other features, such as the 'Dragon who makes men beasts', it is reminiscent of F6 and its Demon. MacNeice in his preface prophesied that pure 'realism' was played out, and his folk-tale outline, with the youngest son destined to go out against the Dragon, as had his vanished father and elder brothers before him, takes its conventions for granted, not attempting to explain them realistically. The language too is often uncompromisingly poetic, as when hero and heroine vye with each other in describing the sea, like any Shakespearian couple:

> The sea today is drunken marble . . .
> The sea today is silver stallions. (DT 47)

Other passages are like Eliot, in the characteristic use of the abstract noun and definite article that so many of the younger poets imitated, consciously or otherwise:

> Forward through the gibbering guile of the forest,
> Forward through the silent doubt of the desert.
> (DT 55)

And a more colloquial style is also incorporated into the verse:

> Oh this desert.
> The forest was bad enough, but this beats all. (DT 56)

Along with the acceptance of convention, the medium of radio itself gives a certain freedom, for instance in making scene changes – here Benjamin Britten's 'Dark Tower theme' music indicates transitions – and another freedom was that other verbal effects, such as the repeated 'Tick, Tock' and 'Left, Right' that accompany part of the final journey through the desert can be used for atmosphere without the writer having to put bodies to his speakers and work out who, how many and where they should be. The climax of the play is a version of the basic problem of *Murder in the Cathedral*, here divested of its religious application, in that the completion of the quest must be willed freely, not undertaken through fear, coercion, emotional blackmail or early conditioning. The power of the radio to speak inside the listener's head was less used in his subsequent prose plays, and some critics felt that the oral poet's need for a quick effect had not had a good influence on his poetic style generally.

Nonetheless radio drama seems an admirable vehicle for plays which demand attention to the words, and a regular but sparse supply of verse plays is broadcast to the present day, as well as revivals of bygone verse plays such as Byron's *Cain* and *Manfred*. Dorothy Sayers, for example, wrote a memorable cycle of plays for the radio: particularly memorable, it seems, to the production staff of the BBC who suffered her perfectionist requirements on casting and other aspects.

However the most famous poetic radio drama after the war was written in prose – *Under Milk Wood.* Dylan Thomas wrote various pieces of poetic prose about that fertile subject, his Welsh childhood, sometimes with an overflowing excess that appears to justify T. S. Eliot's misgivings about poetic prose having to be too poetic all the time. His narrative broadcast *Reminiscences of Childhood* launches enthusiastically into a description of 'an ugly lovely town (or so it was, and is, to me) crawling, sprawling, slummed, unplanned, jerry-villa'd and smug-suburbed by the side of a long and splendid curving shore', there seems no reason why he should ever stop. However, in another piece, *Return Journey*, he contains his lyrical descriptions within crisper dialogue, a technique he develops further in *Under Milk Wood* (1954) itself.

Apparently Thomas considered writing a stage play before this, for he wrote in a letter:

> I was working on a play, mostly in verse. This, I have reluctantly and, I hope, only temporarily, abandoned; the language was altogether swamping the subject: the comedy, for that was what it was originally intended to be, was lost in the complicated violence of the words: I found I was labouring at each line as though I were making some savage and devious metaphysical lyric and not a play at all. So I set the hotchpotch aside and am prepared to wait.

> But out of my working, however vainly, on it, came . . . the idea that I write a piece, a play, an impression for voices, an entertainment out of the darkness, of the town that I live in.[1]

The 'metaphysical' play may never have existed outside Thomas's imagination but his next broadcast, *Quite Early One Morning*, seems to have been a trial run for *Under Milk Wood*. A framing 'plot' (outlined at length by Daniel Jones's *Preface* to the text) involving a mock trial of the eccentric town for insanity, was never used, and for the final version of *Under Milk Wood* Thomas returned to the idea of 'an impression', the only structure given by the progress of one day, from pre-dawn darkness to dusk again. A main character, blind Captain Cat, shares the narration with two other voices, who describe the town, alternating the change of viewpoint or simply to vary the voice timbre. They also give 'stage directions' such as 'Says Mr. Pugh, and quick as a flash he ducks her in rat soup' (UMW 63) – this, of course, is Mr. Pugh's fantasy about his hated wife, and thus is more than a real stage direction could tell or show.

The dialogue varies from extended passages such as the one between the Pughs, who have quite a miniature scene to themselves, to the mosaic of short speeches from different characters, briefly introduced by the narrators, as they dream, in the morning, the afternoon, or settle for the night. Characteristic of the romanticism of the play is Captain Cat's recollection of old acquaintances, a sentimental poignancy running through the nostalgia as we are reminded that they are all dead; his beloved Rosie Probert whispers 'Come on up, boys, I'm dead' while the next speaker immediately counteracts any seriousness by making death into a joke – 'come to a bad end, very enjoyable' (UMW 4). The play is a comedy and the language insists on this. Raymond Williams's accusation that Fry's language worked by the refusal of the noun could be adapted to cover Thomas's habit of refusing the noun by interposing nouns twisted into adjectives: this stylistic feature of Thomas's earlier descriptive passages predictably appears in the opening of *Under Milk Wood* too – the girls in their dreams are 'bridesmaided', the boys said 'jollyrodgered' seas, the dogs lie in 'wetnosed' yards. The pace then speeds up and becomes less static as a crop of nouns-as-verbs usher in the morning 'forty-winking . . . neddying . . . dickybird-watching'. But, as in *Return Journey*, this lavishness is kept to its own place in the speeches of the narrators, while the dialogue of the characters is smartly articulate without being extravagant. Mrs Organ Morgan demolishes the promiscuous Polly Garter's excuse about birdnesting with men friends, breathlessly and pertinently:

> And when you think of all those babies she's got, then all I can say is she'd better give up bird nesting that's all I can say, it isn't the right kind of hobby at all for a woman that can't say No even to midgets. (UMW 64)

and Captain Cat is ready with a well-turned witticism, persiflage still being, as Yeats said, a form of creativity open to the average man:

> Careful now, she swabs the front glassy. Every step's like a bar of soap. Mind your size twelveses. That old Bessie would beeswax the lawn to make the birds slip. (UMW 39)

They do not, however, rival their fellow Celts in the

plays of Synge or O'Casey for more lyrical fights of fancy – these are hived off into the narrative speeches.

The question as to whether *Under Milk Wood* is poetic drama or merely 'an entertainment' – if this matters – rests partly on the element of static narrative. Unlike the descriptive passages in for example Shakespeare's plays, those in *Under Milk Wood* are not supplementing the main action with the sort of description dramatists have always used, but rather supplementing narrative with vocal illustrations. The play has in fact been performed on stage, initially even before its first broadcast, and many times since then, and the crucial test that it works on the radio and also on stage confirms what the reader must feel – that the play is an interaction or 'play' of voices, not a mere reading. The narrative is supplemented in another way by verse and ballads. Lily Smalls holds a verse dialogue with herself in front of the wash house mirror; the Reverend Eli Jenkins offers morning and evening doggerel poems to his beloved town, and the schoolchildren, Polly Garter and Mr Waldo sing ballads, of which Thomas had intended to include more: this mixture of different styles and especially their segregation into separate areas – the opposite of the smooth seamless gear-changing that Eliot aimed at – relates Thomas to the younger generation of dramatists whose work he did not live to see.

On the other hand, those who did not mix their styles achieved as much intensity and concentration in their prose dialogue as in Thomas's poetic prose, which makes the distinction between language laid out in separate lines, as usual in verse, and language printed continuously an artificial one. This is particularly obvious with dramatists who tend to write in short lines of dialogue. For instance the interrogation from Pinter's *The Birthday*

Party (1958), like Julia's interrogation quoted above in *The Cocktail Party*, has its own rhythm:

GOLDBERG: Where was your wife?
STANLEY: In –
GOLDBERG: Answer.
STANLEY: (*turning*, *crouched*) What wife?
GOLDBERG: What have you done with your wife?
MCCANN: He's killed his wife!
GOLDBERG: Why did you kill your wife?
STANLEY: (*sitting*, *his back to the audience*) What wife?
MCCANN: How did he kill her?
GOLDBERG: How did you kill her?[2]

Similarly, in Beckett's *Waiting for Godot* (1956) there is a much quoted passage which begins

ESTRAGON: All the dead voices.
VLADIMIR: They make a noise like wings.
ESTRAGON: Like leaves.
VLADIMIR: Like sand.
ESTRAGON: Like leaves.
(*Silence*)
VLADIMIR: They all speak together.
ESTRAGON: Each one to itself.
(*Silence*)
VLADIMIR: Rather they whisper.
ESTRAGON: They rustle.
VLADIMIR: They murmur.
ESTRAGON: They rustle.
(*Silence*)[3]

The passage goes on in this style for some time, alternating the two voices, and alternating discussion of the 'dead voices' with descriptions of their sound, the sections being separated by the silences. This is a musical structure which is as highly wrought as most verse, as the director Peter Hall pointed out:

> I actually believe that Beckett and Pinter are poetic dramatists in the proper sense of the word: they have a linear structure and a formal structure which you'd better just observe – don't learn it wrong, don't speak it wrong, you can't, you mustn't.[4]

Plays all in verse, on the other hand, seem still to be liked by non-English dramatists. Wole Soyinka sometimes writes in verse which his characters speak as dialogue, within realistic settings and situations, as in *The Lion and the Jewel* (1963), but he also uses verse as one of a number of less realistic techniques including dance and simultaneous staging, as in *Kongi's Harvest* (1965). Derek Walcott, whose plays use various verse forms, such as the short unrhythmic lines with half-rhymes in *O Babylon* (1979), considers that Jamaican is a highly melodic language but, like Soyinka, has chosen not to imitate conversation exactly, however melodic, but to impose the additional shaping of verse upon that language.

Several poets came indirectly to poetic drama through translation of older verse plays: Tony Harrison's *Oresteia* (1981) and *The Mysteries* (1985) produced at the National Theatre were a *tour de force*; the *Oresteia* in particular demanded extreme concentration from the audience, the masks of the speakers offering no help from facial expression in taking in the harsh, compressed language Harrison had devised to convey Aeschylus's elaborate, crabbed Greek.

Similarly Ted Hughes, who had written some radio

plays for children in verse, moved to the stage by adapting a translation of Seneca's *Oedipus* (1968) for director Peter Brook, an adaptation that the first translator, David Thomas, generously characterised as 'electrifying'. Brook's production was visually spectacular, beginning with actors strapped to pillars and balcony round the auditorium intoning and humming to produce an inarticulate, directional music, and concluding with a dance round a huge gold phallus. Following this, Hughes went with Brook to Persia in 1971 at the invitation of the Persian government to evolve a play on the Prometheus theme for the celebrations at Persepolis.

This play was *Orghast*, and Orghast is also the name of the invented language in which most of the play is written, in which 'orghast' means light. The idea was to compose a language which by onomatopeia and sound-symbolism would convey its meaning through its sound, as existing languages do not. From arguably sound bases, such as the root 'Gr-' for 'eat' because it causes the mouth to make eating movements, one soon comes to the realm of symbolism for less concrete concepts, such as the orghast–light equivalent. Most of the Orghast dialogue was in short lines, which may or may not be verse – a new language calls into question the definition of verse itself – though the other non-Orghast passages were in Greek and Latin verse and ancient ceremonial Persian. This must represent the ultimate stage in the poet's aspiration to control language absolutely. Because of the 'foreignness' of the text, much of the impact of the performance came from visual elements – the basic oppositions of dark and light, tyranny and freedom, enacted outdoors against the dark rock with fire and lights – and Brook suggested that it was in fact easier for spectators to listen for longer to the musical effect of words they did not understand: Eliot's religious festival audience effect carried to extremes.

Hughes, then, was doing something quite different from other modern verse dramatists, though there may be some similarity of general direction with Yeats's quest for a totally new dramatic sound through chanting, or the incantatory language of some of the surrealists. However, the major dramatist to use verse after the 1950s is John Arden, who has written some plays nearly all in verse, others all prose, but usually mixes verse and prose in the same play, in varying proportions. 'I have always been interested in experiments with verse and prose', he says, 'I think that the assumption that a play must be exclusively one or the other is a very limiting one' and, he went on, the mixture should be obvious and undisguised:

> Yes, I prefer to make a firm distinction. I see prose as being a more useful vehicle for conveying plot and character relationships, and poetry as a sort of comment on them. I find it difficult to carry this out in practice. Brecht, for instance, is usually very, very distinct between the two. I haven't always found it possible to be so. I mean, you are writing a scene for instance, which seems to call for prose, then you get a heightened emotion, and before you know where you are, the prose has become lyrical, and yet it doesn't seem to warrant a change into verse. . . . I think the use of formal verse, and straightforward vernacular prose in juxtaposition is quite a good solution even in a modern play. If people are speaking formal verse with lines that rhyme, the audience does not have to worry whether it sounds natural or not. They are talking poetry. It's with the half and half thing that one is in trouble. (TW 42)

This is a fascinatingly apposite example of another practising dramatist's experience and opinion to set against Eliot's eventual rejection of mixing verse and prose; Arden does not, of course, have to trouble with unpoetic verse, but he has the corresponding problem of over-poetic prose. Interestingly, he arrives at his views by instinct and practice, not by setting up a theory beforehand. Arden went on experimenting in his plays, without becoming stereotyped or lapsing into conventional realism. *The Happy Haven* (1960) used masks and occasional passages of verse; *Live Like Pigs* (1958) had a ballad verse sung at the beginning of each modern naturalistic scene; *The Waters of Babylon* (1957), set in a modern London slum, contained quite a lot of blank verse dialogue; *Armstrong's Last Goodnight* (1964) had the historical Scots mediaeval poet David Lindsay as a major character, and he and others occasionally speak in verse, both this and the prose dialogue being in an invented dialect to give the effect of mediaeval Scottish speech without being totally incomprehensible; *The Hero Rises Up* (1968), a satiric play on the career of Nelson, is full of songs, and uses placards and narration to impose an ironic dimension upon the action; *The Workhouse Donkey* (1964), dealing with local government corruption in an industrial town, has music for its songs and as a background, and mixes very colloquial prose with various kinds of verse – a laconic, clipped blank verse soliloquy for the austere Chief Constable, a rhetorical, formal Shakespearian soliloquy for the gentleman brewer. *Serjeant Musgrave's Dance* (1959), still Arden's best known play, has most of its verse as ballads sung by the characters, though sometimes they recite, as though quoting, other strongly rhymed verse. As Arden says, they are very definitely 'talking poetry'. Clear outlines and strong colours are evident in this story of Victorian serjeant and three men 'on the run, in red uniforms, in a black-and-white coalfield' (SMD 29). Musgrave and his men are not really recruiting but are obsessed with the mission of telling a strike-bound, snow-bound mining town about the horrors of 'a Colonial war'. They have come here because the similar reprisal killings in that war, which have propelled all of them to their strange flight, were triggered off by the death of Billy Hicks, a soldier from this town.

Arden began with the idea of three scenes in his mind, the first being the soldiers' mysterious arrival in the town. The second was the 'stable scene', a scene showing simultaneously the three soldiers bedded down in the stable and the serjeant's bedroom above in the pub. Their whispering, quarrels and dreams – especially when Musgrave shouts in his sleep, 'Burning. Burning. . . . I'm on duty woman. I'm timing the end of the world' (SMD 64) – is reminiscent of Fry's *Sleep of Prisoners* (Arden had mentioned an early liking for Fry). The ballad sung by the youngest soldier Sparky

> She came to me at midnight
> With the moonshine on her arms (SMD 58)

which ends 'So fell my fatal crime', comes just before the arrival of Annie the barmaid (and Billy's deserted sweetheart), and the sequence ends in the accidental death of Sparky himself in a scuffle between the men, unwittingly predicted in his song. The foreboding atmosphere of the plot, set in the first scene by Sparky's song of

> Court martial, court martial they held upon me,
> And the sentence they passed was the high gallows tree.

culminates in the third pivotal scene, in the market place, when Serjeant Musgrave turns his 'recuiting meeting' into a public denunciation of war, hauling Billy's skeleton up on to the market lamp, then threatening his captive audience with the gatling gun. 'Twenty-five to die', he says, to make them remember the message. This scene starts in prose; and Arden explains:

> Some people might have thought that Musgrave's speech in the market place would be a suitable occasion to use verse. I did not, because at that point he has to present a certain amount of factual information concerning the massacre and so forth. Moreover, he is doing it in the role of a recruiting sergeant. Now, a recruiting sergeant who speaks verse is a little awkward. What I needed was an ordinary recruiting speech, written in almost a pastiche style, which then gradually, without the audience quite realizing when, takes on a different meaning. If Musgrave had suddenly broken off and started talking verse too soon, it would have been wrong. As it is, I go into rhymed verse for the episode one calls his dance – although in fact, in the production it was hardly a dance, but a physical and verbal 'demonstration'. (TW 43)

One of Arden's points here is the same as Eliot makes about Becket's sermon. The justification is not necessarily cast-iron in either case – the unacceptability of verse for sermon or recruiting speech should rest on the same grounds as its acceptability in other speeches. But in terms of how Arden wanted the scene to develop, he felt instinctively 'it would have been wrong'. Similarly, when he goes on

> I did use verse in the first act, where Annie is asked what she thinks of soldiers, and she goes off into a four-stanza spoken ballad. There she was speaking on a subject which is actually the theme for the whole play; she is also speaking out of an emotional pressure, and therefore can drop into verse without any difficulty at all. (TW 43)

the 'theme' element seems valid, and in keeping with his other practice, while the 'emotional pressure', corresponding to Eliot's 'emotional intensity' criterion, is interesting but not a 'rule' for a play where emotional pressure often does not lead to verse and where verse does not always indicate 'emotional pressure'.

Watching the play, one feels that the verse is there because of the way the scene is developing rather than automatically triggered by a rise in the emotion content alone. Musgrave's demonstration fails, the dragoons arrive in town, also in scarlet, and the last scene shows Musgrave and Attercliffe, the survivors, in the town gaol, where Attercliffe sings a ballad that explains it is not for soldiers to force an end to war:

> I plucked a blood-red rose-flower down
> And gave it to my dear . . .
>
> Your blood-red rose is withered and gone
> And fallen on the floor:
> And he who brought the apple down
> Shall be my darling dear. (SMD 103)

Arden had said that ballads were 'the bedrock of English poetry' and saw them as having a dramatic clarity very different from the faint half-tones of the conventionally 'poetic' which the young Yeats had regretted:

> in the ballads the colours are primary. Black is for death, and for the coalmines. Red is for murder, and for the soldier's coat the collier puts on to escape from his black. Blue is for the sky and for the sea that parts true love. Green fields are speckled with bright flowers. The seasons are clearly defined. White winter, green spring, golden summer, red autumn.[5]

Under the red, white, black, green colours of the ballads, there is great underlying complexity – as the mistaken simplicity of Musgrave's idea of ending violence bears witness. A typical dramatic moment in the play, with interaction of different effects at different levels, is Annie's lament over Billy's skeleton:

> My true love is a scarecrow
> Of rotted rag and bone
> Ask him: were are the birds, Billy?
> Where have they all gone?
>
> He says: Unbutton my jacket, and they'll fly out of the ribs. (SMD 95)

The song is not artless, it is self-conscious, in its enigmatic image of birds as lost life. Annie sees herself as a ballad character, fated 'to sit here making up song-ballads' and by commenting on this as she conforms to the image, she asserts the immediacy and reality of her experience.

Where other writers have used verse, they have usually followed Arden (and Brecht) in separating it from the other prose dialogue and often as part of a non-naturalistic presentation of the subject matter. A contemporary of Arden, Charles Wood, for instance, set his *H* in nineteenth-century Imperial India: he gives his hero verse speeches as well as prose dialogue, and also uses tableaux and painted curtains to stress the artificiality of the theatrical medium and of the play's situation. Later dramatists have similarly come to write verse passages in their plays, approaching it in different ways. Edward Bond is a writer whose plays often include highly poetic prose speeches, such as those of the trial scene in his *Lear* (1971), and he has always produced poems on the same subject as his plays, written concurrently with them but published separately. When writing about poets, he only provided poems within the play for the Japanese Basho – perhaps understandably, given the invidious prospect of writing verse masterpieces for Shakespeare, the hero of his *Bingo* (1973). But in *Restoration* (1981) Bond inserted several songs, with an amplified pop band accompanying them, between the scenes, in which the characters comment in a detached and critical way upon the social and historical situation which within the plot they cannot see. Others among his later, shorter plays also use verse, and in a letter quoted by David L. Hirst, Bond thought that in drama 'poetry should be a creation of "natural signs"' and claimed that 'literature always aspires to the lyric'.[6] Conversely, Howard Brenton in *The Romans in Britain* (1980) lets his dialogue occasionally slide into a passage of gnomic one-sentence lines which effectively is a verse form but is not necessarily cut off from the rest of the prose speeches. Another intentionally parodic use of verse decorates Stephen Berkoff's bizarre satire, *Decadence*, in 1981, which deflated his gross and empty-headed modern targets not only by Berkoff's own baroque performance in the major male roles but also by the incongruous echoes of the verse of revenge tragedy.

The position in the second half of the twentieth century, then, is that the all-verse play has become rare, and certainly is no longer taken as belonging to any school or movement, however vaguely defined. John Arden's brief all-verse *Ars Longa Vita Brevis* (1963) was not classed as a development in satirical verse drama, and Soyinka's plays were not related to those of Eliot's generation or to the past achievements of Western poetic drama, but were seen as the unique production of this individual playwright. The position of verse in drama is just one of a very varied range of theatrical styles which co-exist simultaneously. This co-existence is the significant feature: most of these non-naturalistic styles have appeared in various productions from the turn of the century onwards but, like the Poetic Drama Movement, have tended to occur in temporary waves and phases, and usually in small peripheral theatres. But in the second half of the twentieth century theatre has moved to a more eclectic position – audiences now accept illusion-breaking techniques in commercial productions, not just in those Eliot dismissed as 'late imitation of "experimental theatre"'. Thus a dramatist writing now is free to choose from among these techniques without fear of limiting himself to the avant-garde or festival audience; and one of the techniques he can – but need not – choose is verse dialogue. One would not speak of a 'prose drama movement' because, apart from the assumption that prose is the norm, even for tragedy, it would cover too many unrelated genres to be meaningful. Similarly, poetic drama did originally define itself against prose drama, but always included very varied kinds of verse, as well as differing subject matter and themes. The struggle of poetic drama for acceptance is over – defeated, if seen as a struggle for dominance; but the evolution of modern theatrical writing and performance has found a place for verse in drama, where each different use of verse is judged on its own terms and its own merits.

Abbreviations

(Editions as specified in full in the Bibliography.)

Yeats

E	*Explorations* (W. B. Yeats)
JH	*Joseph Holloway's Abbey Theatre* (eds Hogan and O'Neill)
L	*The Letters of W. B. Yeats*
V	*The Variorum Edition of the Plays of W. B. Yeats* (ed. Russell K. Alspach)

Eliot

CPP	*The Complete Poems and Plays of T. S. Eliot*
EMB	*The Making of T. S. Eliot's Plays* (E. Martin Browne)
R	*The Rock* (T. S. Eliot)
SE	*Selected Essays* (T. S. Eliot)
SP	*Selected Prose* (T. S. Eliot)
3VP	*The Three Voices of Poetry* (T. S. Eliot)

Auden/Isherwood

DD	*The Dance of Death* (Auden)
F6	*The Ascent of F6* (Auden and Isherwood)
OF	*On the Frontier* (Auden and Isherwood)

Spender

TJ	*Trial of a Judge* (Spender)

MacNeice

OP	*Out of the Picture* (Louis MacNeice)
DT	*The Dark Tower* (Louis MacNeice)

Duncan

TWT	*This Way to the Tomb* (Ronald Duncan)

Williams

CP	*The Collected Plays of Charles Williams* (ed. Heath-Stubbs)

Fry

(The three volumes of plays issued by OUP are not numbered, but are referred to in roughly chronological order.)

I	*Boy With a Cart, The Firstborn, Venus Observed*
II	*A Phoenix Too Frequent, Thor With Angels, The Lady's Not for Burning*
III	*A Sleep of Prisoners, The Dark is Light Enough, Curtmantle*
YS	*A Yard of Sun* (Fry)
20C	*The Twentieth Century*

Thomas

UMW	*Under Milk Wood* (Dylan Thomas)

Arden/D'Arcy

SMD	*Serjeant Musgrave's Dance* (Arden)
TW	*Theatre at Work* (eds Marowitz and Trussler)

Notes

1. Introduction: Poetic Drama and the Twentieth Century

1. Eliot, T. S., 'The Poetry of W. B. Yeats' in Hull, J. and Steinmann, M. (eds), *The Permanence of Yeats* (New York: Macmillan, 1950), p. 342.
2. Yeats, W. B., *Letters to the New Island* (OUP, 1934), p. 134.
3. Yeats, W. B., *Autobiography*, quoted by Roger Shattuck in *The Banquet Years* (Faber, 1959), p. 161.
4. Eliot, T. S. and George Hoellering, *The Film of Murder in the Cathedral* (Faber, 1952), p. 8.
5. Mendelson, Edward (ed.), *The English Auden* (Faber, 1976), p. 273.
6. Fry, Christopher, 'Poetry and the Theatre', *Adam*, XIX (1951), 8.
7. Yeats, W. B., *Essays and Introductions* (Macmillan, 1961), p. 274.
8. Eliot, T. S., Introduction to Bethell, S. L., *Shakespeare and the Popular Dramatic Tradition* (Staple Press, 1944) (unnumbered).
9. Mendelson, (ed.), *The English Auden*, p. 273.
10. Ibid., p. 273.

11. Willett, John (ed.), *Brecht on Theatre* (Methuen, 1964), p. 66.
12. Ibid., p. 204.

2. Yeats and the Development of his Theory and Practice

1. Gregory, Lady, *Our Irish Theatre* (Putnam, 1913), pp. 6–7.
2. Moore, George, *Ave* (Heinemann, 1914), p. 99.
3. In Yeats, *Essays and Introductions*.
4. Moore, *Ave*, p. 90.
5. Yeats, W. B., *Autobiographies* (Macmillan, 1955), p. 416.
6. Yeats, *Essays and Introductions*, p. 101.
7. Fay, Frank and Catherine Carswell, *The Fays of the Abbey Theatre* (New York: Harcourt, Brace, 1935), p. 208.
8. Yeats, *Essays and Introductions*, p. 101.

3. Later Yeats: The Noh Plays and After

1. Taylor, Richard, 'Assimilation and Accomplishment', in O'Driscoll, Robert and Lorna Reynolds (eds), *Yeats and the Theatre* (Macmillan, 1975), p. 137.
2. Ibid., p. 139.
3. Ibid., p. 139.

4. Eliot: 'Murder in the Cathedral' and its Predecessors

1. Bennett, Arnold, *The Journals of Arnold Bennett* (Penguin, 1954), p. 376.
2. Worth, Katharine, 'Eliot and the Living Theatre', in Martin, Graham (ed.), *Eliot in Perspective* (Macmillan, 1970), p. 154.
3. Smith, Stevie, 'History or Poetic Drama?' in Braybrook, Neville (ed.), *T. S. Eliot: a Symposium for his Seventieth Birthday* (Rupert Hart-Davis, 1958), p. 173.
4. Eliot and Hoellering, *The Film of Murder in the Cathedral*, p. 8.

5. Later Eliot: 'The Family Reunion', 'The Cocktail Party' and his Other Modern Plays

1. Kenner, Hugh, *The Invisible Poet* (Routledge & Kegan Paul, 1959), p. 339.
2. Worth, in *Eliot in Perspective*, p. 159.
3. Theatre programme, August 1979.
4. Barry, Michael, 'Televising *The Cocktail Party*', in *T. S. Eliot: A Symposium for his Seventieth Birthday*, p. 86.
5. In Jones, David E., *The Plays of T. S. Eliot* (Routledge & Kegan Paul, 1960).

6. Poetic Drama in the Thirties

1. Unpublished interview for *Time* magazine with T. G. Foote (1963), quoted in Carpenter, Humphrey, *W. H. Auden: A Biography* (George Allen and Unwin, 1981), p. 152.
2. Isherwood, Christopher, *Christopher and his Kind* (Methuen, 1977), p. 180.
3. Carpenter, *W. H. Auden: A Biography*, p. 225.
4. Spender, Stephen, *The Thirties and the Arts* (Fontana, 1978), p. 55.
5. Bottomley, Gordon, *A Stage for Poetry* (Kendal: 1948), p. xiv.
6. Ibid., p. xiii.
7. Ibid., p. 69.

7. Christopher Fry: Poetic Drama in Conventional Setting

1. Donoghue, Denis, *The Third Voice* (OUP, 1959), p. 183.
2. Fry, Christopher, *An Experience of Critics* (Perpetua, 1952), p. 183.
3. Ibid., pp. 26–7.
4. Ibid., p. 26.
5. Donoghue *The Third Voice*, p. 182.
6. Fry, Christopher, *Death is a Kind of Love* (Tidal Press, 1979) (unnumbered).
7. Ibid.

8. Fry, Christopher, 'Venus Considered', *Theatre Newsletter*, IV, no. 93 (11 March 1950), 5.
9. Ibid., p. 5.
10. Tynan, Kenneth, *He That Plays the King* (Longmans, 1950), p. 144.

8. New Directions in Poetic Drama: the Position Today

1. Fitzgibbon, (ed.), *Selected Letters of Dylan Thomas*, p. 364.
2. Pinter, Harold, *The Birthday Party* (Methuen, 1981), p. 49.
3. Beckett, Samuel, *Waiting for Godot* (Faber, 1956), p. 6.
4. Hall, Peter, interviewed by Catherine Itzin and Simon Trussler, 'Directing Pinter', *Theatre Quarterly*, 16 (1975), 4.
5. Arden, John, 'Telling a True Tale', *Encore*, no. 25 (1960), 24.
6. Hirst, David, *Edward Bond* (Macmillan, 1985), p. 159.

Select Bibliography

(Place of publication London, unless otherwise stated.)

PRIMARY SOURCES

(i) Introduction
Willett, John (ed.), *Brecht on Theatre* (Methuen, 1964)

(ii) Yeats
A Variorum Edition of the Plays of W. B. Yeats (ed. Russell K. Alspach, assisted by Catherine Alspach) (Macmillan, 1966)
Collected Plays of W. B. Yeats (Macmillan, 1952)
The Letters of W. B. Yeats (Rupert Hart-Davis, 1954)
Autobiographies (Macmillan, 1955)
Essays and Introductions (Macmillan, 1961)
Explorations (Macmillan, 1962)

(iii) T. S. Eliot
Complete Poems and Plays (Faber, 1969)
The Rock (Faber, 1934 – this play has not been republished and is generally unavailable)
Selected Essays (Faber, 1934)

Selected Prose (ed. John Hayward) (Penguin in association with Faber, 1953)
The Three Voices of Poetry (Cambridge University Press, 1953)
The Use of Poetry and the Use of Criticism (Faber, 1933)

(iv) Fry

Plays (*Boy With a Cart*, *The Firstborn*, *Venus Observed*) (Oxford University Press, 1970)
Plays (*A Phoenix Too Frequent*, *Thor With Angels*, *The Lady's Not for Burning*) (Oxford University Press, 1969)
Plays (*A Sleep of Prisoners*, *The Dark is Light Enough*, *Curtmantle*) (Oxford University Press, 1971)
A Yard of Sun (Oxford University Press, 1970)
An Experience of Critics (Perpetua, 1952)

(v) Poetic Drama in the Thirties

Auden, W. H., *Collected Longer Poems* (Faber, 1974)
Auden, W. H., *The Dance of Death* (Faber, 1933)
Auden, W. H. and Christopher Isherwood, *The Dog Beneath the Skin* (Faber, 1935)
Auden, W. H. and Christopher Isherwood, *The Ascent of F6* (Faber, 1937)
Auden, W. H. and Christopher Isherwood, *On the Frontier* (Faber, 1938)
Duncan, Ronald, *This Way to the Tomb* (Faber, 1946)
MacNeice, Louis, *Out of the Picture* (Faber, 1937)
Spender, Stephen, *Trial of a Judge* (Faber, 1938)
Williams, Charles, *Collected Plays of Charles Williams* (ed. John Heath-Stubbs) (Oxford University Press, 1963)

(vi) Afterwards

Arden, John, *Three Plays* (*The Waters of Babylon*, *Live like Pigs*, *The Happy Haven*) (Penguin, 1969)
Arden, John, *Serjeant Musgrave's Dance* (Methuen, 1960)
Arden, John, *The Workhouse Donkey* (Methuen, 1964)
Arden, John, *Armstrong's Last Goodnight* (Methuen, 1965)
Arden, John and Margaretta D'Arcy, *The Hero Rises Up* (Methuen, 1971)
Arden, John, *To Present the Pretence* (Methuen, 1977)

MacNeice, Louis, *The Dark Tower and other Radio Scripts* (Faber, 1947)
Soyinka, Wole, *Collected Plays*, vols I and II (Oxford University Press, 1974)
Thomas, Dylan, *Under Milk Wood* (Dent, 1962)
Thomas, Dylan, *Miscellany One* (Dent, 1963)
Bond, Edward, *Theatre Poems and Songs* (eds Malcolm Hay and Philip Roberts) (Methuen 1978)
Wood, Charles, *H* (Methuen, 1970)

SECONDARY SOURCES

(i) General Books on Poetry in Drama

Fergusson, Francis, *The Idea of a Theatre* (New York: Doubleday, 1949)
Hinchcliffe, Arnold, *Modern Verse Drama* (Methuen, 1977)
Kennedy, Andrew, *Six Dramatists in Search of a Language* (Cambridge University Press, 1975)
Lloyd-Evans, Gareth, *The Language of Modern Drama* (Dent, 1977)

(ii) European Background

Benson, Renate, *German Expressionist Drama* (Macmillan, 1984)
Esslin, Martin, *The Theatre of the Absurd* (Penguin, 1968)
Knapp, Bettina, *French Theatre 1918–1939* (Macmillan, 1985)
Schumacher, Claude, *Alfred Jarry and Guillaume Apollinaire* (Macmillan, 1984)
Sokel, Walter H., *The Writer in Extremis* (Stanford: Stanford University Press, 1959)

(iii) Yeats

Ellis-Fermor, Una, *The Irish Dramatic Movement* (Methuen, 1967)
Fay, Frank and Catherine Carswell, *The Fays of the Abbey Theatre* (New York: Harcourt, Brace, 1935)
Holloway, Joseph, *Joseph Holloway's Abbey Theatre* (eds Hogan and O'Neill) (Carbondale, 1967)
Miller, Liam, *The Noble Drama of W. B. Yeats* (Dublin: Dolmen Press, 1977)

Moore, George, *Ave* (Heinemann, 1914)
O'Driscoll, R. and Lorna Renolds, *Yeats and the Theatre* (Macmillan, 1975)
Worth, Katharine, *The Irish Drama of Europe* (Athlone Press, 1978)

(iv) T. S. Eliot

Braybrook, N. (ed.), *T. S. Eliot: A Symposium for his Seventieth Birthday* (Rupert Hart-Davis, 1958)
Browne, E. Martin, *The Making of T. S. Eliot's Plays* (Cambridge University Press, 1969)
Hinchliffe, Arnold P. (ed.), *T. S. Eliot: Plays* (Casebook) (Macmillan, 1985)
Jones, D., *The Plays of T. S. Eliot* (Routledge & Kegan Paul, 1960)
Martin, Graham, *Eliot in Perspective* (Macmillan, 1970)
Worth, Katharine, *Revolutions in Modern English Drama* (Bell, 1972)

(v) Poetic Drama in the Thirties

Carpenter, Humphrey, *W. H. Auden, A Biography* (George Allen and Unwin, 1981)
Isherwood, Christopher, *Christopher and his Kind* (Methuen, 1977)
Mendelson, Edward (ed.), *The English Auden* (Faber, 1976)
Spender, Stephen, *The Thirties and the Arts* (Fontana, 1978)

(vi) Fry

Stanford, Derek, *Christopher Fry: An Appreciation* (Peter Nevill, 1951)
Stanford, Derek, *Christopher Fry* (Longmans, 1954)

(vii) Later Writers

Gray, Frances, *John Arden* (Macmillan, 1982)
Hunt, Albert, *Arden: A Study of his Plays* (Methuen, 1974)
Hirst, David L., *Edward Bond* (Macmillan, 1985)
Marowitz, Charles, and Simon Trussler (eds) *Theatre at Work* (Methuen, 1967)

Index

Index